Pacific Coast
= Highway =

Pacific Coast = Highway =

ALICE STARMORE

The
Broad Bay
Company

Credits

COPYRIGHT OF TEXT & KNITWEAR DESIGN © ALICE STARMORE 1997 APART FROM *FORT ROSS, POINT REYES & SAND DOLLAR* © JADE STARMORE 1997 **NOT TO BE KNITTED FOR RESALE** STRICTLY NO UNAUTHORISED RE-PRODUCTION **PUBLISHED BY** THE BROAD BAY COMPANY, PO BOX 2935, FORT BRAGG CA 95437, USA. DIRECTORS DAVID CODLING, ALICE STARMORE **DISTRIBUTED BY** UNICORN BOOKS & CRAFTS, INC. 1338 ROSS STREET, PETALUMA CA 94954, USA PHONE 707–762–3362 FAX 707–762–0335

ISBN 0–9625586–7–2

FASHION PHOTOGRAPHY PATRICK McHUGH **STYLIST** BIRTE WALTER **HAIR AND MAKE-UP** SHAWN MCFARLAND **MODELS** RAELYN BOCKBRADER, JASON COTTER, AJ HITCHCOCK **CHILD MODELS** REMINGTON & SPENCER MARTIN, GRACE RODERICK **GRAPHIC DESIGN & PRODUCTION** THE WINDFALL PRESS, ISLE OF LEWIS, SCOTLAND **KNITTING ILLUSTRATIONS & CHARTS** JADE STARMORE AT WINDFALL PRESS **COLOUR REPRODUCTION & PRINTING** THE DAI NIPPON PRINTING CO (HK) LTD **THE BROAD BAY KNITTERS** JEAN DOWNTON, MARGARET FINLAYSON, CHRISSIE MACLEOD, JOAN MACLEOD, MARGARET MACLEOD, MARGARET NICOLSON, BETTY SEDDON, MORAG STEWART **SPECIAL THANKS TO** ALEXANDRA BOCKBRADER, NANCY DENKIN & LOUISE SPANGLER **TO ONE AND ALL** HAPPY TRAILS.

GALLERY OF CONTENTS

P24 Little Boxes

P28 Abalone

P46 Fort Ross

P56 Russian River

P62 Sand Dollar

P72 Point Reyes

P86 Mendocino

P92 Super Skunk

P76 Point Arena

P80 Irish Beach

P98 Noyo Harbor

P102 Glass Beach

CALIFORNIA
1

Foreword

Those who regularly follow my work will know that the sea is right at the top of my list of influences, closely followed by landscape. They will also know of – and perhaps take some amusement from – my fascination with the American road; its atmosphere and images, and the endless variations in light and colour that it presents.

In PACIFIC COAST HIGHWAY I have managed to combine all of these favourite themes by drawing on images from the stretch of Highway I between San Francisco and Fort Bragg. The Broad Bay Company has just moved from New Jersey to Fort Bragg, and it was an ideal opportunity to explore its new and dramatic Californian surroundings, from which I have picked out features of seascape, landscape and architecture to serve as sources for this thematic collection.

One new aspect of this collection is the fact that it includes three designs from the apprentice who has been working with me for the past year. I felt that it was time to take on an apprentice, and I planned a four year programme that was completely within the rigorous and hard-working spirit of the trade and craft apprenticeships that used to be such a vital part of British industry, and which have so sadly died away in recent years. The programme combines knitting technique and practice; design mathematics, and a judicious amount of the routine labour involved in the finishing of knitted garments to perfection. On seeing the programme, my daughter – whose training so far has been in art and graphic design – surprised me by asking if she could take on the job. She has made rapid progress and has quickly developed her own design style. The three pieces that form her end-of-year assignments are included here, and I hope that knitters will find them of technical and aesthetic interest.

In keeping with The Broad Bay Company's commitment to excellence of product and to timeless knitting design, I have sought to provide a range of projects which are stimulating to make – both for the novice and the dedicated expert – and a pleasure for all to wear.

Alice Starmore

Golden Gate

SIZES

To fit chest/bust 86-99[102-114]cm 34-39[40-45]in.
Directions for larger size are given in square brackets. Where there is only one set of figures, it applies to both sizes.

KNITTED MEASUREMENTS

Underarm 124[135]cm 49[53]in.
Length 70[73.5]cm.
Sleeve length 44cm.

MATERIALS

12[13] Skeins of **Bainin**, shown in Brick and Turf.
1 Pair each 4mm (US 6) and 5mm (US 8) needles.
1 Set of double-pointed or short circular 4mm (US 6) needles. 1 Cable needle. 4 stitch holders. Stitch markers.

STITCHES

Chart Patts: On flat pieces, odd numbered rows are RS and are read from right to left, and even numbered rows are WS and are read from left to right. On circular rnds (Chart A only), all rows are RS and are read from right to left.
Note: The stitch count in chart C varies due to the Blackberry stitch fillings inside the diamond panels. The "blackberries" are increased from 1 to 3 sts each on WS rows, and then decreased from 3 to 1 sts on following WS rows. This means that the stitch count inside the diamonds will increase until all the blackberries within the diamond are completed.

TENSION

18 Sts and 22 rows to 10cm, measured over st.st. using 5mm (US 8) needles.

BACK

** With pair of 4mm (US 6) needles, cast on 138[145] sts. Work the patt from chart A as follows—
Row 1 (RS): Reading from right to left, rep the 7 patt sts 19[20] times; patt the last 5 sts as indicated.
Row 2 (WS): Reading from left to right, patt the first 5 sts as indicated; rep the 7 patt sts 19[20] times.
Continue as set and rep the 2 patt rows until piece measures 8[9]cm from cast on edge, with WS facing for next row.
Next Row – Inc
First Size; Patt 9; * m1, patt 5; rep from * to the last 9 sts; m1, patt 9. 163 sts.
Second Size: Patt 5; (m1, patt 5) 5 times; (m1, patt 4) 21 times; (m1, patt 5) 5 times; m1; patt 6. 177 sts.
Both Sizes
Change to 5mm (US 8) needles, beg at row 1 of charts and set the patt as follows—
Row 1 (RS): Reading from right to left, work chart B over the first 14[21] sts, repeating the 7 patt sts 2[3] times; work

chart C over the next 135 sts, repeating the 60 patt sts twice, then work the first 15 sts of patt once more; work chart D over the last 14[21] sts, repeating the 7 patt sts 2[3] times.
Row 2 (WS): Reading from left to right, work chart D over the first 14[21] sts, repeating the 7 patt sts 2[3] times; work chart C over the next 135 sts, working the last 15 sts, then rep the 60 patt sts twice; work chart B over the last 14[21] sts repeating the 7 patt sts 2[3] times. ***
Continue as set and rep all rows of charts, working 154[159] rows in total, thus ending on row 14[19] inclusive of chart C.
Second Size Only: Patt 1 more row, thus working row 20 of chart C, but omitting the incs inside diamond panels so that the st count is 135 over chart C sts.
Both Sizes
Keeping continuity of patt as far as possible, cast off 56[62] sts at beg of next 2 rows, and during cast off, dec 1 st over each 2 st cable and 2 sts evenly over the diamond panels. Place the rem 51[53] centre back sts on a holder.

FRONT

As back from ** to ***. Continue as set and rep all rows of charts, working 140[146] rows in total, thus ending on row 28[6] inclusive of chart C, with RS facing for next row.
Shape Front Neck
Patt the first 64[70] sts (not counting blackberry inc sts on second size) as set; place the next 35[37] sts (centre front) on a holder; leave the rem sts on a spare needle. Turn and shape left side of neck as follows—
+ Keeping continuity of patt as far as possible, dec 1 st at neck edge of next 4 rows. Patt 1 row without shaping, then dec 1 st at neck edge of next and every foll alt row 4 times in all. 56[62] sts rem (not counting blackberry inc sts). Patt 1 row without shaping, and on second size, omit blackberry incs on last row. Cast off sts, decreasing 1 st over 2 st cables, and 2 sts evenly over diamond panels during cast off. ++
With RS facing, rejoin yarn to sts on spare needle and keeping continuity, patt to end of row. Shape RS of neck as left from + to ++.

SLEEVES

With 4mm (US 6) needles, cast on 47[54] sts. Work the patt from chart A as follows—
Row 1 (RS): Reading from right to left, rep the 7 patt sts 6[7] times; patt the last 5 sts as indicated.
Row 2 (WS): Reading from left to right, patt the first 5 sts as indicated; rep the 7 patt sts 6[7] times.
Continue as set and rep the 2 patt rows until cuff measures 6cm from cast on edge, with WS facing for next row.
Next Row – Inc
First Size: * M1, patt 2; rep from * to the last st; m1; patt 1. 71 sts.
Second Size: Patt 1; (m1, patt 3) 5 times; (m1, patt 2) 9 times; (m1, patt 3) 6 times; m1; patt 2. 75 sts.
Both Sizes
Change to 5mm (US 8) needles, beg at row 1 of chart C and set the patt as follows—

Row 1 (RS): Reading from right to left, beg at 33rd [31st]st of chart C and patt the last 28[30] sts of rep; patt the first 43[45] sts of rep.

Row 2 (WS): Reading from left to right, beg at 18th[16th] st and patt the last 43[45] sts; patt the first 28[30] sts.

Continue as set and inc 1 st at each end of next and every foll 3rd row, and on first size work the inc sts into chart C patt until there are 75 sts, then work all foll inc sts into chart B patt on the right, and chart D patt on the left. On second size, work all inc sts into chart B patt on the right, and chart D patt on the left.

Both Sizes: Continue as set until there are 97[101] sts, then continue and inc as set on every foll 4th row until there are 123[127] sts. Continue as set without further shaping until sleeve measures 44cm from cast on edge, with RS facing for next row. **Note:** Omit any blackberry incs on the diamond panels at each side, on last WS row.

Shape Saddle

Cast off 54[56] sts at beg of next 2 rows, decreasing over cables and diamond panels as before. 15 Centre diamond panel sts rem (not including blackberry inc sts).

Continue in patt as set over the centre diamond panel sts until saddle fits in length along shoulder cast off edges. **Note:** Omit any blackberry incs on last WS row, thus ending with 15 sts. Place sts on a holder.

FINISHING

Do not press. Block out pieces, right side up, to measurements shown on schematic. Cover with damp towels and leave to dry. Place markers at each side of back and front, 22[23]cm down from shoulder cast off. Sew saddles along shoulder cast off edges. Sew tops of sleeves to back and front between markers. Press seams very lightly on the WS, using a warm iron and damp cloth. Use the edge of the iron to press the seams only, thus avoiding contact with the garment pieces. Sew up side and sleeve seams and press as before, omitting ribs.

Collar

With RS facing and set of double-pointed or circular 4mm (US 6) needles, beg at back neck holder and pick up and dec sts from holder as follows—

K 3[2]; (k2tog, k 9[6]) 4[6]times; k2tog; k 2[1] – 46 sts rem from holder.

Pick up and dec from left saddle as follows—

K2; (k2tog, k3) twice; k2tog; k1 – 12 sts rem from holder; knit up 12 sts evenly along left side of neck.

Pick up and dec from front neck holder as follows—

k 5[2]; (k2tog, k 10[6]) 2[4] times; k2tog; k 4[1] – 32 sts rem from holder; knit up 12 sts evenly along right side of neck; pick up and dec from right saddle as as left to complete the rnd. 126 sts.

Place a marker at beg of rnd and reading **all** rnds from right to left (all rnds are RS), beg at row 1 of chart A and rep the 7 patt sts 18 times in the rnd. Continue as set until collar measures 12cm. Cast off sts in patt and dec 1 st over 2st cables during cast off.

Darn in loose ends.

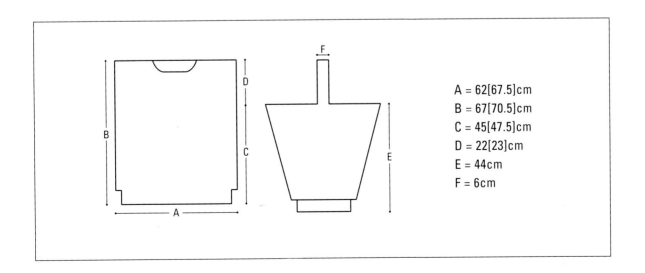

A = 62[67.5]cm
B = 67[70.5]cm
C = 45[47.5]cm
D = 22[23]cm
E = 44cm
F = 6cm

KEY

▬ p on RS rows; k on WS rows.

│ k on RS rows; p on WS rows.

⌐ k into back of st on RS rows; p into back of st on WS rows.

sl first st to cn and hold at back; k1; k1 from cn.

sl first st to cn and hold at front; k1; k1 from cn.

sl first 2 sts to cn and hold at back; k2; p2 from cn.

sl first 2 sts to cn and hold at front; p2; k2 from cn.

sl first 3 sts to cn and hold at back; k2b; sl the p st from cn back onto left needle and p it; k2b from cn.

sl first 2 sts to cn and hold at front; k1; k2b from cn.

sl first st to cn and hold at back; k2b; k1 from cn.

(WS) sl first st to cn and hold at front; p next st; p the st from cn.

(WS) p into front of second st, then p into front of first st and sl both sts off needle together.

sl first st to cn and hold at back; k2b; p1 from cn.

sl first 2 sts to cn and hold at front; p1; k2b from cn.

sl first 2 sts to cn and hold at front; p3; k2 from cn.

sl first 3 sts to cn and hold at back; k2; p3 from cn.

⌄3 k1, p1, k1 into SAME st, thus making 3 sts from 1.

△ p3tog.

sl first 2 sts to cn and hold at back; k2; k2 from cn.

sl first 2 sts to cn and hold at front; k2; k2 from cn.

sl first 2 sts to cn and hold at front; p1, k1b; then k2 from cn.

sl first 2 sts to cn and hold at back; k2; then k1b, p1 from cn.

sl first 2 sts to cn and hold at front; p1, k1b, p1; then k2 from cn.

sl first 3 sts to cn and hold at back; k2; then p1, k1b, p1 from cn.

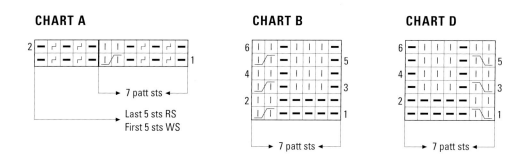

CHART A

CHART B

CHART D

7 patt sts

Last 5 sts RS
First 5 sts WS

7 patt sts

7 patt sts

CHART C

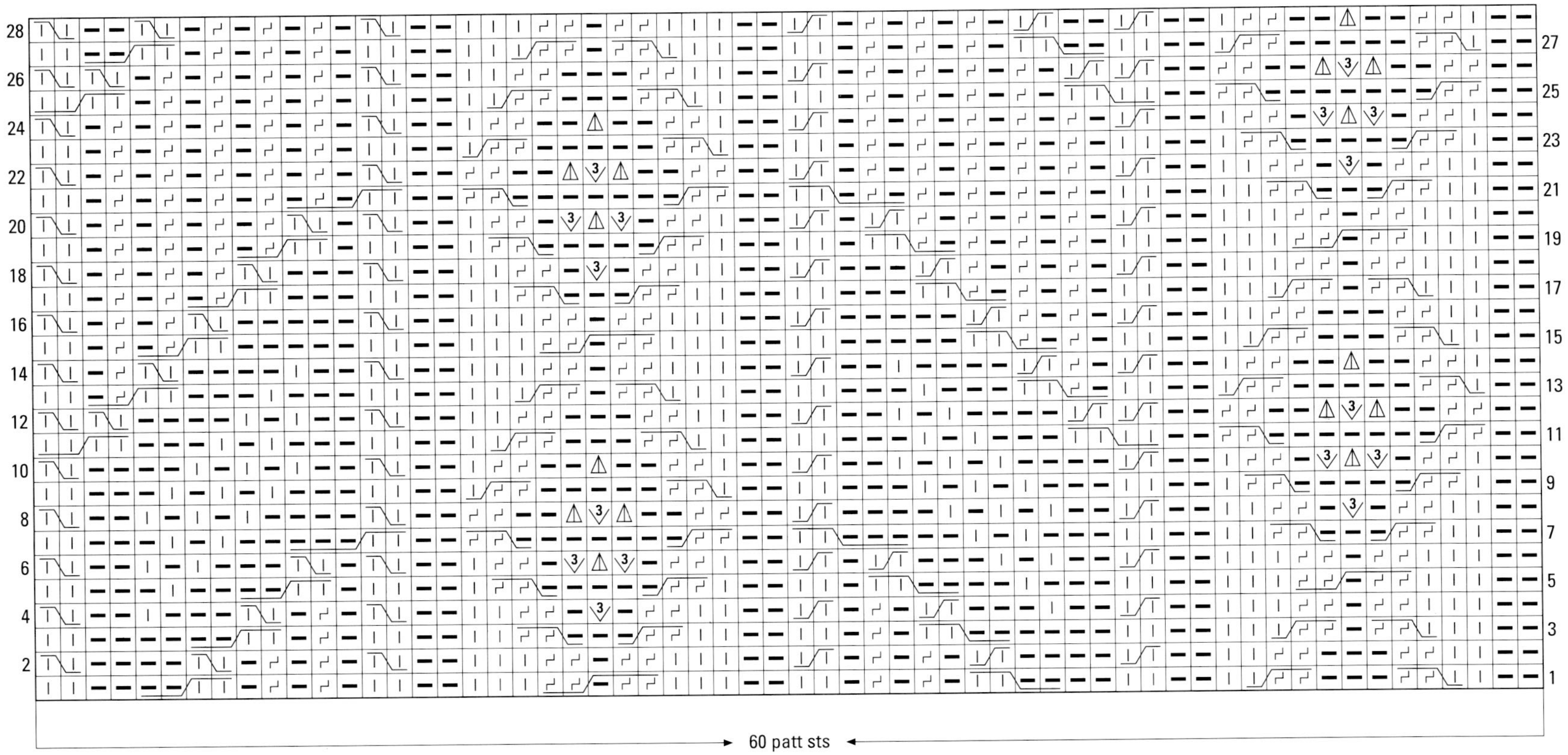
28
26
24
22
20
18
16
14
12
10
8
6
4
2
27
25
23
21
19
17
15
13
11
9
7
5
3
1
60 patt sts

Grant Avenue

CHART A

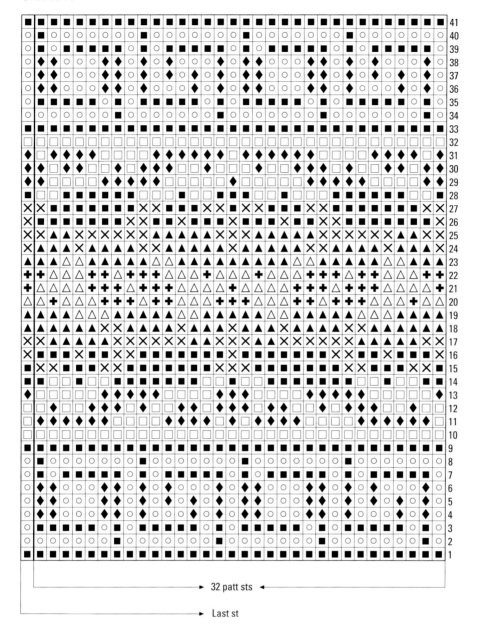

→ 32 patt sts ←

→ Last st

KEY

■	CLARET
○	BRACKEN
◆	RUBY
□	TURQUOISE
✕	DELPH
▲	CARMINE
△	NIGHT HAWK
✚	CERISE
	BRASS
╱	AEGEAN
●	INDIGO
◡	COBALT

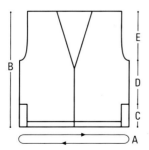

A = 110[115,120]cm
B = 57.5[60,63.5]cm
C = 15cm
D = 19.5[21,23.5]cm
E = 23[24,25]cm

SIZES

To fit bust 81-86[89-94,97-102]cm 32-34[35-37,38-40]in. Directions for larger sizes are given in square brackets. Where there is only one set of figures, it applies to all sizes.

KNITTED MEASUREMENTS

Underarm (buttoned) 110[115,120]cm 43.5[45,47]in. Length 57[60,63.5]cm.

MATERIALS

Of **Scottish Campion** —
4 Skeins of Bracken.
2 Skeins each of Delph, Cobalt and Brass.
1[2,2] Skeins each of Indigo and Night Hawk.
1[1,2] Skeins of Aegean.
1 Skein each of Claret, Ruby, Turquoise, Carmine, Cerise.
1 Set of double-pointed or circular 3.25mm (US 3) needles.
3 Stitch holders. Stitch markers. 7 Buttons.

STITCHES

Check Patt: K2 with first colour, k2 with second colour, stranding the yarns evenly across the WS. On flat rows, every row is worked in k, and on circular rnds, every alt rnd is worked in p. It is important to remember to strand the yarn on the WS after every p2. **Chart Patts:** All rnds are read from right to left. K every rnd, stranding the yarn not in immediate use evenly across the WS. **Steeks:** Worked at front, side openings, armholes and neck, and later cut up centre to form openings. Each steek is worked over 8 sts and k on every rnd. On two-colour rnds the steek sts are worked in alt colours on every st and rnd. Do not weave in newly joined in or broken of yarns at the centre of front steek. Instead leave approx 5cm tail when joining in and breaking off yarns. **Edge Stitch:** Worked at each side of steeks and k in background colours throughout. Sts for front, armhole bands and side edgings are knitted up from edge sts. **Cross Stitch:** With darning needle, overcast raw edges of trimmed steeks to strands on the WS. After sewing to end, reverse to form cross stitches.

TENSION

30 Sts and 34 rows to 10cm, measured over chart patt using 3.25mm (US 3) needles. To make an accurate tension swatch, cast on 33 sts on 1 double-pointed or circular needle and work a flat piece, **knitting on the RS only**, and breaking off the yarns at the end of every row.

BODY

With 3.25mm (US 3) needles and Delph, cast on 320[336,352] sts. Place a marker at beg of rnd and making

---

CHART B

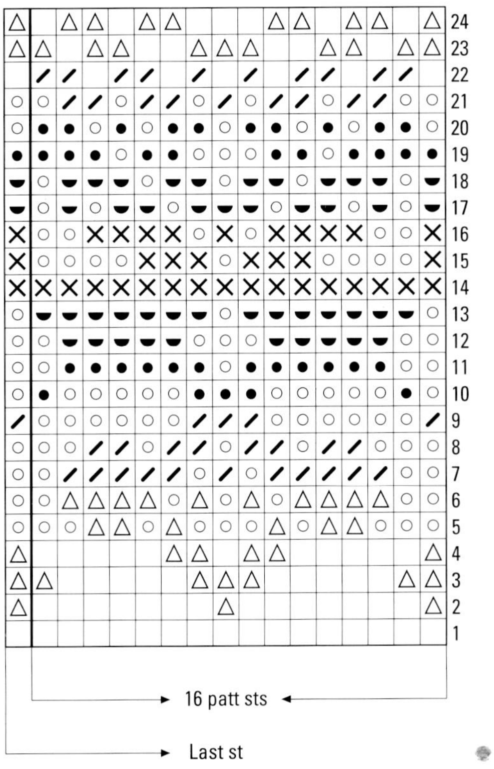

← 16 patt sts →

→ Last st

CHART C

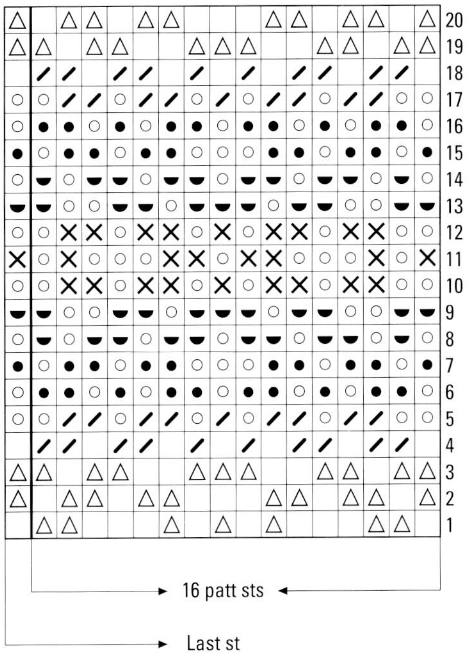

← 16 patt sts →

→ Last st

sure cast on edge is not twisted, join in Bracken and set the front and side steeks, edge sts and check patt as follows—

Rnd 1: With alt colours k4 steek sts; with Delph k1 edge st; (k2 Delph, k2 Bracken) 18[19,20] times over the 72[76,80] right front sts; with Delph k1 edge st; with alt colours k8 steek sts; with Delph k1 edge st; (k2 Delph, k2 Bracken) 36[38,40] times, then k2 Delph over the 146[154,162] sts of back; with Delph k1 edge st; with alt colours k8 steek sts; with Delph k1 edge st; (k2 Bracken, k2 Delph) 18[19,20] times over the 72[76,80] left front sts; with Delph k1 edge st, with alt colours k4 steek sts.

Rnd 2: K4 steek sts and k1 edge st as set; (p2 Delph, p2 Bracken) over the 72[76,80] right front sts; k 10 edge and steek sts as set; (p2 Delph, p2 Bracken) 36[38,40] times, then p2 Delph, over the 146[154,162] sts of back; k 10 edge and steek sts as set; (p2 Delph, p2 Bracken) over the 72[76,80] left front sts; k1 edge st and k4 steek sts as set.

Rnds 3 & 4: As rnds 1 &2 but substitute Cobalt for Bracken and Bracken for Delph and work edge sts in Cobalt.

Rnds 5 & 6: As set, Substituting Indigo for Bracken and Bracken for Cobalt and work edge sts in Indigo.

Rnds 7 & 8: As rnds 3 & 4.

Rnds 9 & 10: As rnds 1 & 2.

Break off yarns. With Claret k 1 rnd and inc 1 st at centre of back. 147[155,163] sts in back and 321[337,353] sts in rnd. Join in Bracken and beg at rnd 2 of chart A and set the patt as follows—

With alt colours k4 steek sts; with Claret k1 edge st; reading from right to left, rep the 32 patt sts twice; patt the first 8[12,16] sts of rep; with Claret k1 edge st; with alt colours k8 steek sts; with Claret k1 edge st; beg on 24th[20th,32nd] st of chart and patt the last 9[13,1] sts of rep; rep the 32 patt sts 4[4,5] times; patt the first 10[14,2] sts of rep; with Claret k1 edge st; with alt colours k8 steek sts; with Claret k1 edge st; beg at 26th[22nd,18th] st of chart and patt the last 7[11,15] sts of rep; rep the 32 patt sts twice; patt the last st as indicated; with Claret k1 edge st; with alt colours k4 steek sts.

Joining in and breaking off colours as required, continue as set, working all steek sts in alt colours on two-colour rnds, and edge sts in background colours throughout and work through rnd 40 of chart A.

Next Rnd – Cast Off Side Steeks

With Claret, k 1 rnd and cast off the 8 sts of right and left side steeks. Break off Claret.

Next Rnd – Cast on Side Sts

With Brass k the first 78[82,86] sts; cast on 13 sts; k 149[157,165] sts; cast on 13 sts; k the last 78[82,86] sts. 331[347,363] sts.

Join in Night Hawk and beg at rnd 2 of chart B, set the patt as follows—

With alt colours k4 steek sts; with Night Hawk k1 edge st; reading from right to left, rep the 16 patt sts 20[21,22] times in the rnd; patt the last st as indicated; with Night

Hawk k1 edge st; with alt colours, k4 steek sts.

Joining in and breaking off colours as required, continue as set, working the steek sts in alt colours on two-colour rnds, and working the edge sts in background colours throughout and work through rnd 24 of chart B. Then continue to work steek and edge sts as set and beg at rnd 1, work chart C instead of chart B over the patt sts. Rep the 20 patt rnds, working 41[47,55] chart C rnds in total, thus ending on rnd 1[7,15] inclusive.

Next Rnd – Beg Armhole Steeks and V Neck Shaping

With colours as for rnd 2[8,16] of chart C, k4 steek sts and k1 edge st as set; ssk; keeping continuity, patt the next 68[71,74] sts; place the next 19[21,23] sts on a holder (right underarm); cast on 10 steek and edge sts in colours as set at front; keeping continuity, patt the next 143[149,155] sts of back; place the next 19[21,23] sts on a holder (left underarm); cast on 10 steek and edge sts as before; keeping continuity, patt the next 68[71,74] sts; k2tog; k1 edge st and k4 steek sts as set.

Place a marker at each front neck edge st to mark beg of neck shaping. Work armhole steeks and edge sts as front steek and edge sts, and keeping continuity of patt throughout, dec 1 st at chart patt side of armhole edge sts on next 8 rnds, then on every foll alt rnd 8 times in all. 111[117,123] chart patt sts rem on back. AT THE SAME TIME, continue to dec as set at front edge sts on every 3rd rnd. Then continue working armholes without further shaping and continue to dec as set at front edge sts on every 3rd rnd until 28[30,32] chart patt sts rem on each front shoulder. Continue as set without further shaping and work through rnd 19[9,19] of chart, thus working 119[129,139] chart C rnds in total.

Patt the next rnd of chart and edge sts as set and cast off all steek sts on this rnd.

Place centre back 55[57,59] sts on a holder.

With Night Hawk[Delph, Night Hawks] graft front and back shoulder sts together including edge sts.

Armhole Bands

Cut open armhole steeks up centre between 4th and 5th steek sts.

With RS facing, 3.25mm (US 3) needles and Indigo, beg at centre of underarm holder and pick up and k the last 10[11,12] sts from holder; knit up 145[151,153] sts evenly around armhole, working into loop of edge st next to chart patt sts; pick up and k the rem 9[10,11] sts from holder. 164[172,176] sts. Place a marker at beg of rnd, and joining in and breaking off colours as required, work check patt as follows—

Rnd 1: * K2 Indigo, k2 Bracken; rep from * to end of rnd.
Rnd 2: * P2 Indigo, p2 Bracken; rep from * to end of rnd.
Rnd 3: * K2 Bracken, k2 Cobalt; rep from * to end of rnd.
Rnd 4: * P2 Bracken, p2 Cobalt; rep from * to end of rnd.
Rnd 5: * K2 Cobalt, k2 Bracken; rep from * to end of rnd.
Rnd 6: * P2 Cobalt, p2 Bracken; rep from * to end of rnd.
Rnd 7: * K2 Bracken, k2 Delph; rep from * to end of rnd.

Rnd 8: * P2 Bracken, p2 Delph; rep from * to end of rnd. With Delph, cast off knitwise.

Front Band

Cut open front steek up centre between 4th and 5th steek sts.

With 3.25mm (US 3) needles and Indigo, beg at cast on edge of right front, and working into loop of edge st next to chart patt sts, knit up 102[108,115] sts evenly to marker at beg of neck shaping; knit up 69[72,74] sts evenly along right front neck to back neck holder; pick up and k the sts from holder and dec 1 st at centre back – 54[56,58] sts rem from holder; knit up 69[72,74] sts evenly along left front neck to marker; knit up 102[108,115] sts evenly along left front to cast on edge. 396[416,436] sts.

Next Row (WS): With Indigo, k.

Work check patt as follows—

Row 1 (RS): * K2 Indigo, k2 Bracken; rep from * to end of row.

Row 2 (WS): * K2 Bracken, k2 Indigo; rep from * to end of row.

Rows 3 & 4: As rows 1 & 2, substituting Cobalt for Bracken and Bracken for Indigo.

Row 5 – Make Buttonholes: Working in colour sequence beg k2 Cobalt, k2 Bracken and keeping continuity, patt 4[6,6]sts ;* cast off 2, patt 14[14,15]; rep from * 6 times in all; cast off 2; patt straight as set to end of row.

Row 6: With colours and patt as set, cast on 2 sts over those cast off on previous row.

Row 7: * K2 Bracken, k2 Delph; rep from * to end of row.

Row 8: * K2 Delph, k2 Bracken; rep from * to end of row. With Delph, cast off knitwise.

Side Opening Bands

Cut open side steeks up centre between 4th and 5th steek sts.

With RS facing, 3.25mm (US 3) needles and Indigo, beg at cast on edge of left side of openings and knit up 46 sts evenly to top of openings, working into loop of edge st next to chart patt sts. Turn and with Indigo k 1 row. Work 8 rows of check patt in colour sequence as front band, beg and ending all rows with a k2 in same colour. With Delph, cast off knitwise.

With RS facing, beg at top end of right side of openings and knit up 46 sts as previous side, but working to cast on edge. Turn, and with Indigo k 1 row. Work 8 rows of check patt and cast off sts as left side of openings.

FINISHING

Trim all steeks to a 2st width and with Delph, cross stitch steeks in position. Sew top ends of side opening bands to cast on edge of sides. Using a warm iron and damp cloth, press garment lightly on WS, omitting check patt areas. Sew buttons onto left front band.

Little Boxes

To fit approx. age 2-3[4-5,6-7] years, or —
chest 54-56[58-61,63-66]cm 21-22[23-24,25-26]in.
Directions for larger sizes are given in square brackets. Where there is only one set of figures, it applies to all sizes.

KNITTED MEASUREMENTS

Underarm 72[76.5,86.5]cm 28.5[30,34]in.
Length 36[41.5,47]cm.
Sleeve length 22.5[25.5,28]cm.

MATERIALS

Of Scottish Heather –
2[2,3] Skeins each in Scotch Broom and Granny Smith.
1[1,2] Skeins each in Hydrangea and Salmon.
1 Skein each in Lichen and Wilde Mushroom.
1 Pair of 4.5mm (US 7) needles. 1 Set of double-pointed or short circular 4.5mm (US 7) needles.
2 Stitch holders. Stitch marker.
Note: To make a medium sized adult version (approx measurements – underarm 120cm: length 68cm: sleeve length 43cm) you will require 5 skeins of Granny Smith; 4 skeins of Scotch Broom; 3 skeins each of Hydrangea and Salmon; 2 skeins each of Lichen and Wilde Mushroom.

STITCHES

Check Patt: Worked flat in rows on back, front and cuffs. Worked in the round on neckband. K2 with first colour, then k2 with second colour, stranding the yarns evenly across the WS. On flat rows, every row is worked in k, and on circular rnds, every alt row is worked in p. It is important to remember to strand the yarn on the **WS** after every p2 on circular rnds. Make sure not to strand the yarn too tightly. The tension on the check patt should be the same as that of the chart patt areas. **Chart Patt:** Worked entirely in st.st. (k on RS rows, p on WS rows). Odd numbered rows are RS and are worked from right to left. Even numbered rows are WS and are worked from left to right. Use separate lengths of yarn for each area of colour so that there are no strands crossing coloured areas on the WS. Link one colour to the next on every row by crossing the yarn from the last colour worked over the yarn for the next colour, before working the next st.

TENSION

18 Sts and 26 rows to 10cm, measured over chart patt using 4.5mm (US 7) needles.

BACK

** With 4.5mm (US 7) needles and Granny Smith, cast on 62[66,74] sts. Joining in and breaking off colours as required, work Check patt as follows—
Row 1 (RS): * K2 Granny Smith, k2 Hydrangea; rep from * to the last 2 sts; k2 Granny Smith.
Row 2 (WS): As row 1, stranding the yarns across the WS.
Rows 3 & 4: * K2 Salmon, k2 Granny Smith; rep from * to the last 2 sts; k2 Salmon.
Rows 5 & 6: * K2 Scotch Broom, k2 Salmon; rep from * to the last 2 sts; k2 Scotch Broom.
Row 7: * K2 Hydrangea; k2 Scotch Broom; rep from * to the last 2 sts; k2 Hydrangea.
Next Row – Inc
With colours as set, inc as follows—
First & Second Sizes: K2; (m1, k 29[31]) twice; m1; k 2. 65[69] sts.
Third Size: K1; (m1, k 24) 3 times; m1; k 1. 78 sts.
Next Row – Beg Chart Patt
Using separate lengths of yarn for each area of colour, and reading RS rows from right to left, and WS rows from left to right, set the chart patt as follows—
First Size – Row 1 (RS): Rep the 26 patt sts twice; patt the last 13 sts as indicated on chart.
Second Size – Row 1 (RS): Patt the first 2 sts as indicated on chart; rep the 26 patt sts twice; patt the last 15 sts as indicated on chart.
Third Size – Row 1 (RS): Rep the 26 patt sts 3 times. ***
All Sizes: Continue as set and rep the 28 patt rows, working 78[92,106] chart patt rows in total, thus ending on row 22[8,22] inclusive, with RS facing for next row.
Shape Back Neck
Keeping continuity of chart, patt 19[20,23] sts; place the next 27[29,32] sts on a holder for back neck; leave the rem sts on a spare needle. Shape right side of neck as follows—
+ Turn and keeping continuity of patt, dec 1 st at neck edge of next and foll alt row. 17[18,21] shoulder sts rem. Patt 2 rows without shaping, thus ending on row 28[14,28] inclusive. Cast off sts. ++
With RS facing and keeping continuity of chart, patt the 19[20,23] sts of left side, thus ending with WS facing for next row. Shape as right side, working from + to ++.

FRONT

As back from ** to ***.
Continue in patt as set and work 70[84,98] chart patt rows in total, thus ending on row 14[28,14] inclusive, with RS facing for next row.
Shape Front Neck
Keeping continuity of chart, patt 23[24,27] sts; place the next 19[21,24] sts on a holder for front neck; leave the rem sts on a spare needle. Shape left side of neck as follows—
+ Turn and keeping continuity of patt, dec 1 st at neck edge of next and every foll alt row until 17[18,21] sts rem. Patt 2

rows without shaping, thus ending on row 28[14,28] inclusive. Cast off sts. ++
With RS facing and keeping continuity of chart, patt the 23[24,27] sts of right side, thus ending with WS facing for next row. Shape as left side, working from + to ++.

SLEEVES

With 4.5mm (US 7) needles and Granny Smith, cast on 30[32,34] sts. Joining in and breaking off colours as required, work 8 rows of check patt in colour sequence as back and front (**Note:** On second size, omit the last 2 sts on RS rows, then k WS rows in colours as RS rows).
All Sizes – Row 9: * K2 Granny Smith, k2 Hydrangea; rep from * to the last 2[0,2] sts; k2[0,2] Granny Smith.
Second Size Only – Row 10 (WS): * K2 Hydrangea, k2 Granny Smith; rep from * to end of row. **Row 11:** * K2 Hydrangea; k2 Granny Smith; rep from * to end of row.
All Sizes – Inc
With colours as set, k1[1,2]; (m1, k 9[10,10]) 3 times; m1; k 2[1,2]. 34[36,38] sts.
Next Row – Beg Chart Patt
Using separate lengths of yarn for each area of colour, and reading RS rows from right to left, and WS rows from left to right, set the chart patt as follows —
Row 1 (RS): Patt the last 4[5,6] sts of 26 st rep; work the 26 patt sts; patt the first 4[5,6] sts of 26 st rep.
Patt the next (WS) row as set. Continue as set and inc 1 st at each end of next and every foll third row, working increased sts into chart patt, until there are 60[66,72] sts in total. Continue without shaping and work through row 18[24,4] of chart, thus working 46[52,60] chart patt rows in total. Cast off sts.

FINISHING

Darn in all loose ends. Press pieces very lightly on WS (omitting check patt areas), using a warm iron and a damp cloth. Join back and front at shoulder seams. Place centre top of sleeves at shoulder seams and sew sleeves to body. Press seams on WS as before. Sew up side and sleeve seams and press seams as before, omitting check patt areas.
Neckband
With RS facing, set of double-pointed or circular 4.5mm (US 7) needles and Scotch Broom, beg at back neck and pick up and k the 27[29,32] sts from holder; knit up 13[13,14] sts evenly along left side of neck; pick up and k the 19[21,24] sts from front neck holder; knit up 13[13,14] sts evenly along right side of neck to complete the rnd. 72[76,84] sts. Place a marker at beg of rnd and joining in and breaking off colours as required, work check patt as follows—
Rnd 1: * K2 Scotch Broom, k2 Salmon; rep from * to end of rnd. **Rnd 2:** * P2 Scotch Broom, p2 Salmon; (stranding yarn on **WS**) rep from * to end of rnd. **Rnd 3:** * K2 Salmon, k2 Granny Smith; rep from * to end of rnd.
Rnd 4: * P2 Salmon, p2 Granny Smith; rep from * to end of rnd. **Rnd 5:** * K2 Granny Smith, k2 Hydrangea; rep from * to end of rnd. **Rnd 6:** * P2 Granny Smith, p2 Hydrangea; rep from * to end of rnd.
With Granny Smith, cast off knitwise. Darn in loose ends.

CHART

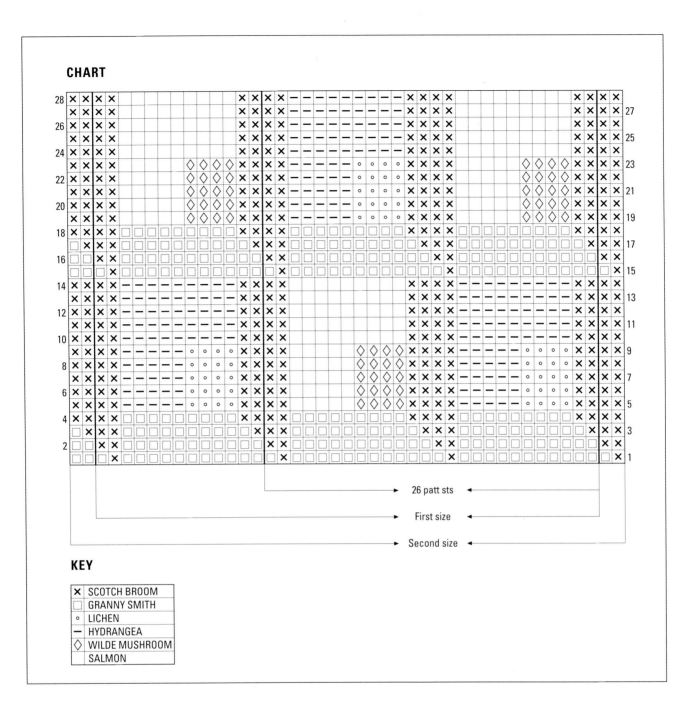

26 patt sts

First size

Second size

KEY

×	SCOTCH BROOM
☐	GRANNY SMITH
○	LICHEN
—	HYDRANGEA
◇	WILDE MUSHROOM
	SALMON

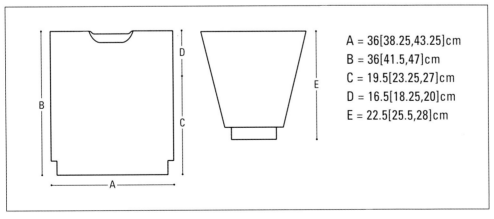

A = 36[38.25,43.25]cm
B = 36[41.5,47]cm
C = 19.5[23.25,27]cm
D = 16.5[18.25,20]cm
E = 22.5[25.5,28]cm

Abalone

SIZES

To fit bust 81-86[91-97,102-107]cm 32-34[36-38,40-42]in. Directions for larger sizes are given in square brackets. Where there is only one set of figures, it applies to all sizes.

KNITTED MEASUREMENTS

Underarm (buttoned) 110[120,131]cm 43.5[47.5,51.5]in.
Length 68.5[72,74]cm.
Sleeve length 43[44.5,46]cm.

MATERIALS

Of **Scottish Campion** —
4 Skeins of Anemone.
3[3,4] Skeins each of Teal, Rosemary and Lilac.
3 Skeins each of Night Hawk and Light Violet.
2[2,3] Skeins each of Sea Green and Dark Green.
2 Skeins of Mauve Mist.
1[1,2] Skeins each of Damson and Aubretia.
1 Set of double-pointed or circular 3.25mm (US 3) needles.
1 Set of short double-pointed 2.75mm (US 2) needles.
3 Stitch holders. 2 Safety pins. 12[13,13] Buttons.

STITCHES

Check Patt: K2 with first colour, k2 with second colour, stranding the yarns evenly across the WS. On flat rows, every row is worked in k, and on circular rnds, every alt rnd is worked in p. It is important to remember to strand the yarn on the WS after every p2. **Chart Patt:** All rnds are read from right to left. K every rnd, stranding the yarn not in immediate use evenly across the WS. **Steeks:** Worked at front, armholes and neck, and later cut up centre to form openings. Each steek is worked over 8 sts and k on every rnd. On two-colour rnds, the steek sts are worked in alt colours on every st and rnd. Do not weave in newly joined in or broken off yarns at centre of front steek. Instead leave approx 5cm tail when joining in and breaking off yarns. **Edge Stitch:** Worked at each side of steeks and k in darker colours on two-colour rnds. Sts for front bands, neckband and sleeves are knitted up from edge st. **Cross Stitch:** With darning needle, overcast raw edges of trimmed steeks to strands on WS, and after sewing to end, reverse to form cross stitches.

TENSION

30 Sts and 34 rows to 10cm, measured over chart patt using 3.25mm (US 3) needles. To make an accurate tension swatch, cast on 33 sts on 1 double-pointed or circular needle and work a flat piece, **knitting on the RS only**, breaking off the yarns at the end of every row.

BODY

With 3.25mm (US 3) needles and Dark Green, cast on 328[360,392] sts. Place a marker at beg of rnd, and making sure cast on edge is not twisted, join in Anemone and set the front steek, edge sts, and check patt as follows—
Rnd 1: With alt colours k4 steek sts; with Dark Green k1 edge st; * k2 Dark Green, k2 Anemone; rep from * to the last 7 sts; k2 Dark Green; with Dark Green k1 edge st; with alt colours k4 steek sts.
Rnd 2: With alt colours k4 steek sts; with Dark Green k1 edge st; * p2 Dark Green, p2 Anemone; rep from * to the last 7 sts; p2 Dark Green; with Dark Green k1 edge st; with alt colours k4 steek sts.
Rnds 3 & 4: As rnds 1 & 2, but substitute Anemone for Dark Green, and Dark Green for Anemone.
Rnds 5 & 6: As set, but substitute Night Hawk for Anemone and Lilac for Dark Green.
Rnds 7 & 8: As set, but substitute Lilac for Night Hawk and Teal for Lilac.
Rnds 9 & 10: As set, but substitute Teal for Lilac and Light Violet for Teal.
Rnds 11 through 16: As set, working colours as rnd 6 back through rnd 1.
Break off Anemone and with Dark Green inc as follows—
K 6; * m1; k 158[174,190]; rep from * once more; m1; k6. 331[363,395] sts. Break off Dark Green.
Next Rnd – Beg Chart Patt
Join in Sea Green and k the first rnd of chart. Join in Damson and working rnd 2 of chart, set the patt as follows—

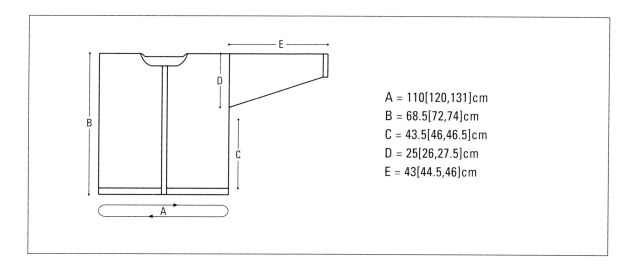

A = 110[120,131]cm
B = 68.5[72,74]cm
C = 43.5[46,46.5]cm
D = 25[26,27.5]cm
E = 43[44.5,46]cm

CHART

KEY

	SEA GREEN
△	DAMSON
✐	AUBRETIA
■	ROSEMARY
○	MAUVE MIST
✕	LIGHT VIOLET
•	TEAL
◇	LILAC
—	NIGHT HAWK
✳	ANEMONE
◆	DARK GREEN

Row numbers (bottom to top): 1, 2, 3, 4, 5, 6, 7, 8, 9, 10, 11, 12, 13, 14, 15, 16, 17, 18, 19, 20, 21, 22, 23, 24, 25, 26, 27, 28, 29, 30, 31, 32, 33, 34, 35, 36, 37, 38, 39, 40, 41, 42, 43, 44, 45, 46, 47, 48, 49, 50, 51, 52, 53, 54, 55, 56, 57, 58

→ 32 patt sts ←

→ Last st

With alt colours, k4 steek sts; with Sea Green k1 edge st; rep the 32 patt sts 10[11,12] times; patt the last st as indicated; with Sea Green k1 edge st; with alt colours k4 steek sts.

Continue as set, working the steek sts in alt colours and the edge sts in background colours on two-colour rnds, and rep the 58 patt rnds, working 134[143,145] chart patt rnds in total, thus ending on rnd 18[27,29] inclusive.

Next Rnd – Beg Armhole Steeks

With colours as for next rnd of chart, k4 steek sts; k1 edge st; keeping continuity, patt 80[88,96] sts (right front); place the next st on a safety pin; cast on 10 sts (the first and last st cast on are edge sts, the centre 8 are steek sts); keeping continuity, patt the next 159[175,191] sts (back); place the next st on a safety pin; cast on 10 edge and steek sts as before; keeping continuity, patt the next 80[88,96] sts (left front); k1 edge st; k4 steek sts.

Continue as set, working armhole steeks in alt colours and edge sts in background colours on two-colour rnds, and continue in patt until 194[206,210] chart patt rnds have been worked from beg, thus ending on rnd 20[32,36] inclusive.

Next Rnd – Beg Front Neck Shaping

With colours as for next rnd of chart, cast off the first 5 sts of rnd (right front steek and edge st); keeping continuity, patt as set to the last 5 sts of rnd and cast off these 5 sts (left front steek and edge st). Break off yarns.

Next Rnd: Place the first 12[13,13] sts of right front neck on a holder; with colours as for next rnd of chart cast on 4 steek sts and 1 edge st and mark the first st cast on for beg of rnd; keeping continuity, patt as set to the last 12[13,13] sts of rnd and place these sts of left front neck on a holder; cast on 1 edge st and 4 steek sts.

Work front neck steek sts in alt colours and edge sts in background colours on two-colour rnds, and keeping continuity, shape front neck by decreasing 1 st at each side of front neck edge sts on next 7 rnds. 61[68,76] chart patt sts rem on each front. Then continue to dec as set on every foll alt rnd 6[6,7] times in all. 55[62,69] chart patt sts rem on each front.

Next Rnd – Beg Back Neck Shaping

Keeping continuity, work straight as set to the 159[175,191] chart patt sts of back; keeping continuity, patt the first 55[62,69] sts; place the next 49[51,53] sts on a holder (back neck); cast on 10 sts (the first and last sts cast on are edge sts, the centre 8 are steek sts); keeping continuity, patt the

rem 55[62,69] sts of back and work straight as set to end of rnd.

Work back neck steek in alt colours and edge sts in darker colours on two-colour rnds, and keeping continuity, dec 1 st at each side of front and back neck edge sts on next and foll alt rnd. 53[60,67] chart patt sts rem on each shoulder. Continue without further shaping, and work through rnd 46[58,6] inclusive, and cast off all steek sts on this last rnd. With Dark Green[Rosemary,Sea Green] graft shoulder sts together including edge sts.

SLEEVES

Cut open armhole steeks up centre, between 4th and 5th steek sts.

With 3.25mm (US 3) needles and Dark Green[Night Hawk,Rosemary] k the st from safety pin and mark this st for beg of rnd and underarm st; knit up 151[157,163] sts evenly around armhole, working into loop of edge st next to chart patt sts. 152[158,164] sts.

Joining in and breaking off colours as required, set the patt as follows—

With background colour colour, k underarm st; beg at rnd 47[44,39] and patt the last 11[14,1] sts of 32 st rep; rep the 32 patt sts 4[4,5] times; patt the first 12[15,2] sts of 32 st rep.

Patt the next 2 rnds as set, working the underarm st in background colour on two-colour rnds.

Next Rnd – Beg Sleeve Shaping

With colours as for next rnd of chart, k underarm st; k2tog in background colour; keeping continuity, patt as set to the last 2 sts; ssk in background colour. Keeping continuity, patt 3 rnds without shaping.

Rep these last 4 rnds until 136[142,144] sts rem, then continue to dec as set on every foll 3rd rnd until 68[72,76] sts rem, thus working 134[137,142] chart patt rnds in total and ending on rnd 6 inclusive.

Change to set of 2.75mm (US 2) needles and work 16 rnds in check patt as body. With Dark Green cast off purlwise.

Neckband

Cut open front and front and back neck steeks up centre, between 4th and 5th steek sts.

With RS facing, 3.25mm (US 3) needles and Teal, pick up and k the 12[13,13] sts from right front neck holder; knit up 29[29,30] sts evenly along right side of neck, working into loop of edge st next to chart patt sts; pick up and k the

49[51,53] sts from back neck holder and dec 1 st at centre back – 48[50,52] sts rem from holder; knit up 29[29,30] sts evenly along left side of neck, working into edge st as before; pick up and k the 12[13,13] sts from left front neck holder. 130[134,138] sts.

Turn and k 1 row. Joining in and breaking off colours as required, and working back and forth in rows, work check patt as follows—

Row 1 (RS): * K2 Teal, k2 Light Violet; rep from * to the last 2 sts; k2 Teal.

Row 2 (WS): As row 1.

Rows 3 & 4: * K2 Lilac, k2 Teal; rep from * to the last 2 sts; k2 Lilac.

Rows 5 & 6: * K2 Night Hawk, k2 Lilac; rep from * to the last 2 sts; k2 Lilac.

Rows 7 & 8: * K2 Anemone, k2 Night Hawk; rep from * to the last 2 sts; k2 Anemone.

Rows 9 & 10: * K2 Dark Green, k2 Anemone; rep from * to the last 2 sts; k2 Dark Green. With Dark Green, cast off purlwise.

Left Front Band

With RS facing, 3.25mm (US 3) needles and Teal, beg at top of neckband and knit up 194[202,206] sts evenly to cast on edge, working into loop of edge st next to chart patt sts. Turn and k 1 row. Work 10 rows in check patt as neckband. With Dark Green, cast off purlwise.

Right Front Band

As left, but beg at cast on edge and knit up 194[202,206] sts to top of neckband, and keeping continuity of check patt, work 12[13,13] buttonholes on 6th row, as follows—

First Size: K6; * cast off 2, k14; cast off 2, k15; rep from * 5 times in all; cast off 2, k14; cast off 2; k5.

Second & Third Sizes: K4[6]; * cast off 2, k14; rep from * 12 times in all; cast off 2, k4[6].

All Sizes – Next Row: Keeping continuity of check patt, cast on 2 sts over those cast off on previous rnd. Complete as left front band.

FINISHING

Trim all steeks to a 2st width and with Teal, cross stitch steeks in position. Darn in all loose ends. Using a warm iron and damp cloth, press garment very lightly on WS, omitting check patt bands. Sew buttons on to left front band.

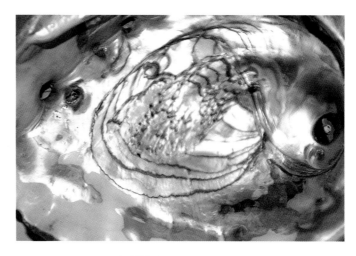

Tiburon

SIZES

To fit age 4-5[6-7,8-9] yrs, or —
chest 58-61[63-66,68-71]cm 23-24[25-26,27-28]in.
Directions for larger sizes are given in square brackets.
Where there is only one set of figures, it applies to all sizes.

KNITTED MEASUREMENTS

Underarm 79[86,92]cm 31[34,36.25]in.
Length 43[47,51]cm.
Sleeve length 26[28,31]cm.

MATERIALS

4[5,6] 100g Hanks of **Bainin** shown in Crimson and French Blue. 1 Pair each 4.5mm (US 7) and 5mm (US 8) needles. 1 Cable needle. 2 Stitch holders. Safety pin.

STITCHES

Moss Stitch: Worked over an odd number of sts as follows—
Rows 1 (RS): P1; * k1; p1; rep from * to end of row.
Rows 2 & 3: K1; * p1; k1; rep from * to end of row.
Row 4: As row 1.
Rep rows 1 – 4.
Chart Patt: Odd numbered rows are RS and are worked from right to left. Even numbered rows are WS and are worked from left to right.

TENSION

19 Sts and 24 rows to 10cm, measured over Moss Stitch using 5mm (US 8) needles.

BACK

** With 5mm (US 8) needles, cast on 75[81,87] sts.
Row 1 (RS): Purl.
Next Row – Inc
K7; * m1; k6; rep from * to the last 8 sts; m1; k8. 86[93,100] sts.
Beg at row 1 of chart and set the patt as follows—
Row 1 (RS): Reading from right to left, rep the 7 patt sts 12[13,14] times; work the last 2 sts as indicated.
Row 2 (WS): Reading from left to right, patt the first 2 sts as indicated; rep the 7 patt sts 12[13,14] times.
Continue as set and rep the 4 patt rows of chart until back measures 26[28,30]cm from cast on edge, with WS facing for next row.
Next Row – Dec
K7; * k2tog; k5; rep from * to the last 9 sts; k2tog; k7. 75[81,87] sts.
Next Row (RS): Purl. ***
Next Row (WS): Purl.
Beg with RS and continue in Moss Stitch until back measures 42[46,50]cm from cast on edge, with RS facing for next row.
Shape Shoulders
P 23[25,27] sts (right shoulder); cast off the next 29[31,33] sts; p the rem 23[25,27] sts of left shoulder. Turn and k the

sts of left shoulder; then turn and cast off sts purlwise.
With WS facing, rejoin the yarn to the sts of right shoulder and k to end of row. Turn and cast off sts purlwise.

FRONT

As back from ** to ***.
Next Row (WS): P 37[40,43] sts and place these sts on a holder (right front yoke); cast off the next st; p the 37[40,43] sts of left yoke and place these sts on a spare needle. Break off yarn.
Begin Collar
With 5mm (US 8) needles cast on 3 sts and patt as follows—
Row 1(RS): K1; p1; k1.
Row 2: (K1, m1) twice; k1. 5 sts.
Row 3: K1; p1; k into back then front of next st making 2 sts on right needle, then insert left needle into vertical strand running between the 2 sts just made and k into this strand, making the third st in the group; p1; k1. 7 sts.
Row 4: K2; p1; k1; p1; k2.
Row 5: K1; p1; k1; m1; p1; m1; k1; p1; k1. 9 sts.
Row 6: K2; p2; k1; p2; k2.
Row 7: K1; p1; k2; m1; p1; m1; k2; p1; k1. 11 sts.
Row 8: K2; p3; k1; p3; k2.
Row 9: K1; p1; sl next 2 sts to cn and hold at back; k1; then k2 from cn; m1; p1; m1; sl next st to cn and hold at front; k2; then k1 from cn; p1; k1. 13 sts.
Row 10: K2; p4; k1; p4; k2.
Row 11: K1; p1; k4; m1; p1; m1; k4; p1; k1. 15 sts.
Row 12: K2; p4; k3; p4; k2.
Row 13: K1; p1; sl next 2 sts to cn and hold at back; k2; k2 from cn; p3; sl next 2 sts to cn and hold at front; k2; k2 from cn; p1; k1.
Row 14: K2; p4; k1 and place these 7 sts on safety pin (right collar); cast off the next st and k1; p4; k2 over rem sts (left collar).
Turn and k1; p1; k4; p1 over left collar sts. Break off yarn.
Work Left Yoke/Collar
Next Row (RS yoke): With 5mm (US 8) needles and RS of front facing, work Moss stitch over the 37[40,43] sts of left front yoke, then with WS of collar facing, work k1; p4; k2 over left collar sts, thus joining WS side of left collar to RS of left yoke. 44[47,50] sts.
Continue as set working the left yoke sts in Moss stitch and the 7 collar sts as set, crossing the cable on the next and every foll 4th row, until left yoke matches back in length at end of Moss stitch, with RS of yoke facing for next row.
Next Row (RS yoke): P 23[25,27] sts; keeping continuity, patt as set over the rem 21[22,23] sts.
Next Row: Patt as set over the first 21[22,23] sts; k 23[25,27].
Next Row: Cast off 23[25,27] shoulder sts purlwise; patt as set to end of row.
Shape top of collar as follows—
Row 1: Patt as set to the last st; yf and sl the last st purlwise; turn.
Row 2: Yf and sl the first st purlwise, thus wrapping yarn round base of slipped st; patt as set to end of row.
Row 3: Patt as set to the last 2 sts; yf and sl the next st purlwise; turn.
Row 4 and All Foll Alt Rows: As row 2.

Row 5: Patt as set to the last 4 sts; yf and sl the next st purlwise; turn.

Row 7: Patt as set to the last 6 sts; yf and sl the next st purlwise; turn.

Row 9: Patt as set to the last 8 sts; yf and sl the next st purlwise; turn.

Row 11: Patt as set to the last 10 sts; yf and sl the next st purlwise; turn.

Row 12: As row 2. Place sts on a holder.

Work Right Yoke/Collar

Place the 7 sts of right collar on a 5mm (US 8) needle so that the tip of the needle is at the inside edge of the collar, then p1; k4; p1; k1 over right collar sts.

Next Row: K2; p4; k1 over collar sts; with RS of front facing, beg with p1[k1,p1] and work Moss stitch over the 37[40,43] sts of right yoke, thus joining WS of collar to RS of yoke. Continue as set and cross the cable on next RS row of collar and continue in patt as set until right yoke matches back in length at end of Moss Stitch, with RS of yoke facing for next row.

Next Row (RS yoke): Keeping continuity, patt as set over the first 21[22,23] sts; p 23[25,27].

Next Row: K 23[25,27]; keeping continuity, patt as set to end of row.

Next Row: Keeping continuity, patt as set over the first 21[22,23] sts; cast off the rem 23[25,27] shoulder sts. Break off yarn. Turn and rejoin yarn to the rem sts and patt to end of row. Then shape collar top as left side, working from row 1 through row 10.

Next Row: Patt as set to the last 10 sts; break off yarn and place all 21[22, 23] sts together on a spare needle.

Sew back and front together at shoulder seams.

Back Collar

With RS of left collar facing, keep continuity and patt as set over left collar sts; with WS of back neck facing, knit up 29[31,33] sts across back neck; with RS of right collar facing, keep continuity and patt as set over right collar sts. 71[75,79] sts in total.

Continue in patt as set, working the back neck sts into Moss stitch, until collar measures 10cm from back neck pick up line, with WS facing for next row. Cast off in patt and dec 1 st at centre of each cable during cast off.

SLEEVES

With 4.5mm (US 7) needles cast on 36[40,44] sts. K1, p1 rib for 5[5.5,6]cm.

Next Row – Inc

Rib 4[5,2]; * m1 rib 3[3,4]; rep from * to the last 5[5,2] sts; m1, rib 5[5,2]. 46[51,55] sts.

Change to 5mm (US 8) needles and work the patt from chart as follows—

Row 1 (RS): Reading from right to left, patt the first 1[0,2] st as indicated; rep the 7 patt sts 6[7,7] times; patt the last 3[2,4] sts as indicated.

Row 2 (WS): Reading from left to right, patt the first 3[2,4] sts as indicated; rep the 7 patt sts 6[7,7] times; patt the last 1[0,2] sts as indicated.

Continue as set and rep the 4 patt rows and inc 1 st at each side of next and every foll 3rd row, working all inc sts into patt, until there are 74[82,91] sts, then continue in patt without shaping until sleeve measures 25[27,30]cm from beg, with RS facing for next row.

Next Row: Purl.

Next Row: Knit.

Cast off sts purlwise.

FINISHING

Darn in yarn ends at collar, sewing centre front and shoulder areas of collar to body. Block pieces to measurements shown on schematic. Place centre top of sleeves at shoulder seams and sew sleeves to body. Press shoulder and sleeve seams lightly on WS. Sew side and sleeve seams, leaving 5[5.5,6]cm openings at each side of hemline.

Make Tassel

Cut 10 lengths of yarn, each 25cm long. Fold in half and attach tassel to centre front collar.

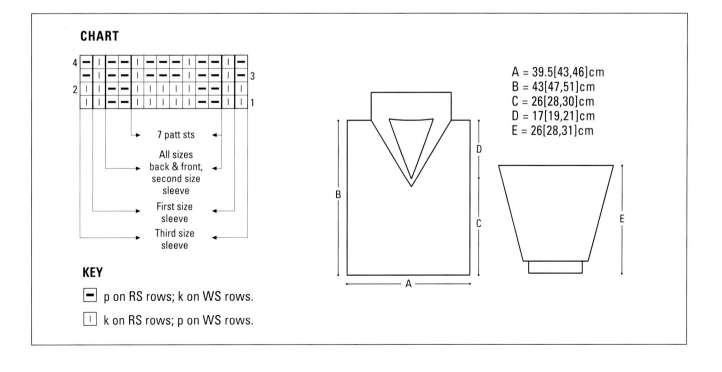

CHART

7 patt sts

All sizes back & front, second size sleeve

First size sleeve

Third size sleeve

KEY

■ p on RS rows; k on WS rows.

□ k on RS rows; p on WS rows.

A = 39.5[43,46]cm
B = 43[47,51]cm
C = 26[28,30]cm
D = 17[19,21]cm
E = 26[28,31]cm

Bodega Bay

SIZES

To fit bust/chest 81-89[91-102,104-112]cm
32-35[36-40,41-44]in.
Directions for larger sizes are given in square brackets.
Where there is only one set of figures, it applies to all sizes.

KNITTED MEASUREMENTS

Underarm 108[116,128]cm 42.5[46,50.5]in.
Length 66[69,72]cm.
Sleeve length 45[46,47]cm.

MATERIALS

12[13,14] 100g balls of **Scottish Fleet**, shown in Teal and Cream. 1 Pair each 2.75mm (US 2) and 3mm (US 3) needles. 1 Set of double-pointed or short circular 3mm (US 3) needles. 1 Cable needle. 4 Stitch holders.

STITCHES

Chart Patts: Odd numbered rows are RS and are read from right to left. Even numbered rows are WS and are read from left to right.

TENSION

35 Sts and 44 rows to 10cm, measured over Chart B patt using 3mm (US 3) needles. To make an accurate tension swatch, cast on 47 sts. Rep the 7 patt sts of chart B, 6 times, then work the first 5 sts of rep. Rep the 2 patt rows 12 times. Do not press the swatch.

FRONT

** With 2.75mm (US 2) needles, cast on 173[187,201] sts. Beg at row 1 of Chart A and set the patt as follows—
Row 1 (RS): Reading from right to left, rep the 7 patt sts 24[26,28] times; patt the last 5 sts as indicated.
Row 2 (WS): Reading from left to right, patt the first 5 sts as indicated; rep the 7 patt sts 24[26,28] times.
Continue as set and rep the 2 rows of chart A until front measures 8cm, with WS facing for next row.

KEY

⊟ p on RS rows; k on WS rows.

⊡ k on RS rows; p on WS rows.

⊟⊟ sl first st to cn and hold at back; k1; k1 from cn.

⊟⊟ sl first st to cn and hold at front; k1; k1 from cn.

⊟⊟⊟⊟⊟ sl first 2 sts to cn and hold at back; k3; then p1, k1b from cn.

⊟⊟⊟⊟⊟ sl first 3 sts to cn and hold at front; k1b, p1; then k3 from cn.

⊟⊟ sl first st to cn and hold at back; k into back of next st; p1 from cn.

⊟⊟ sl first st to cn and hold at front; p1; k into back of st from cn.

⊟⊟ sl first st to cn and hold at back; k1b; k1b from cn.

⊟⊟ sl first st to cn and hold at front; k1b; k1b from cn.

⊟⊟⊟⊟⊟⊟ sl first 3 sts to cn and hold at front; k3; k3 from cn.

⊟⊟⊟⊟⊟⊟ sl first 3 sts to cn and hold at back; k3; k3 from cn.

⊟⊟⊟⊟⊟ sl first 3 sts to cn and hold at front; p2; k3 from cn.

⊟⊟⊟⊟⊟ sl first 2 sts to cn and hold at back; k3; p2 from cn.

[K] make knot thus – (k1, p1) twice into same st, then sl the first 3 sts made over the last st made.

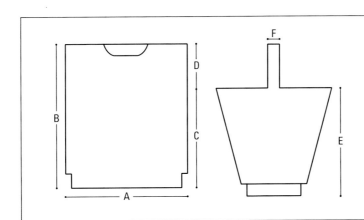

A = 54[58,64]cm
B = 64[67,70]cm
C = 42[44,46]cm
D = 22[23,24]cm
E = 45[46,47]cm
F = 4cm

CHART C

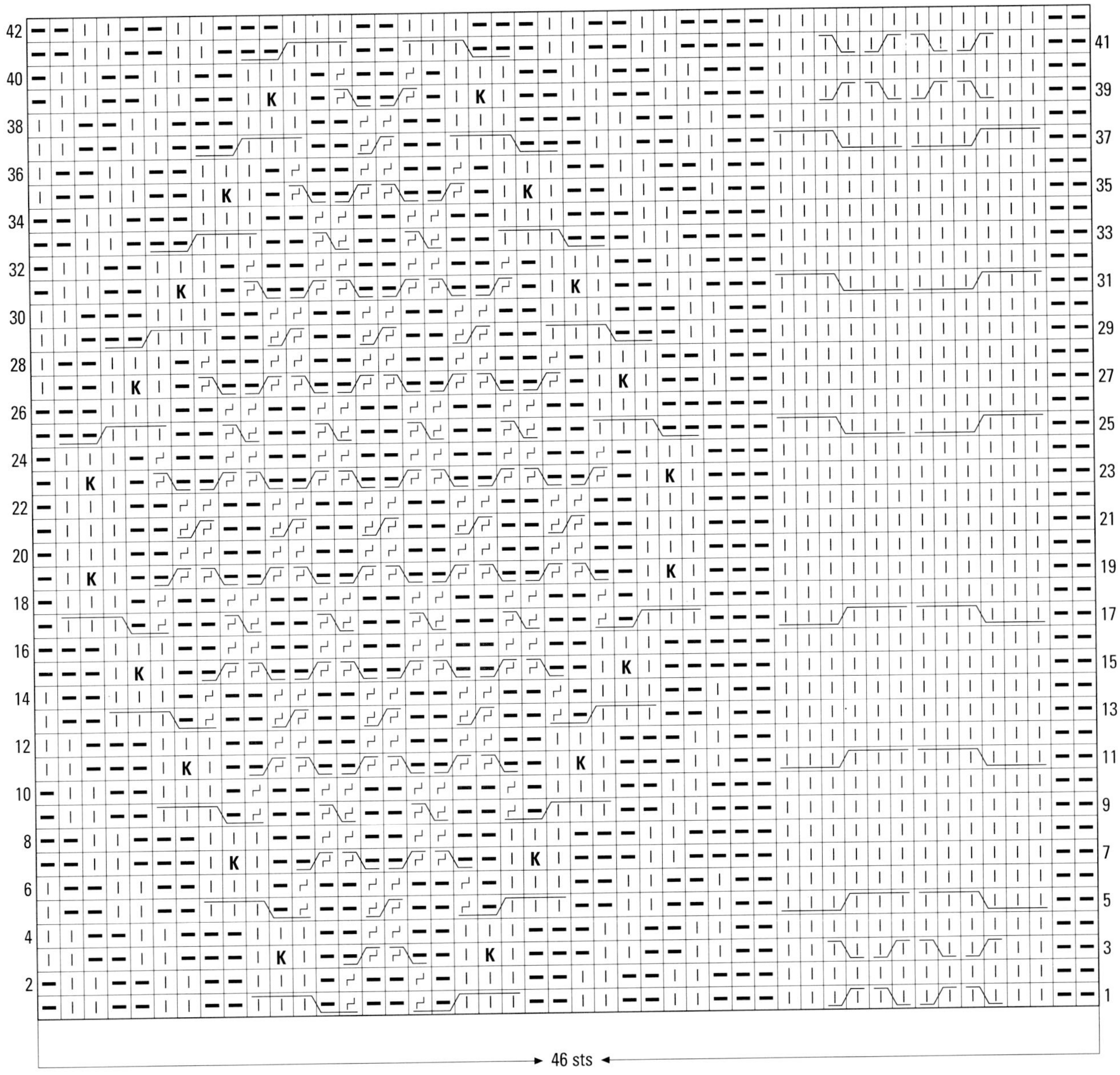

Row numbers (left side, bottom to top): 2, 4, 6, 8, 10, 12, 14, 16, 18, 20, 22, 24, 26, 28, 30, 32, 34, 36, 38, 40, 42

Row numbers (right side, bottom to top): 1, 3, 5, 7, 9, 11, 13, 15, 17, 19, 21, 23, 25, 27, 29, 31, 33, 35, 37, 39, 41

← 46 sts →

CHART A

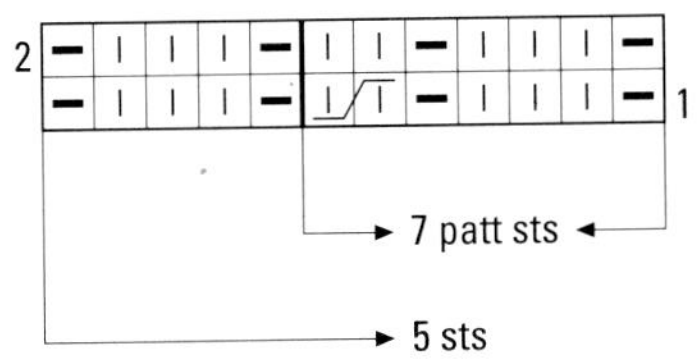

Row numbers: 2, 1

→ 7 patt sts ←

→ 5 sts

CHART B

Row numbers: 4, 3, 2, 1

→ 7 patt sts ←

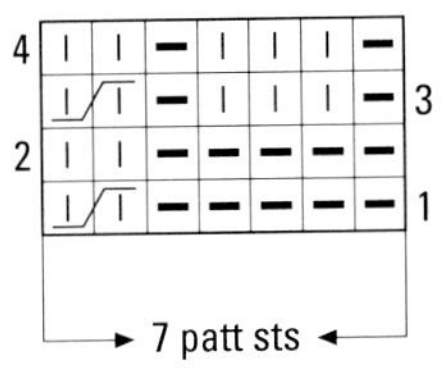

CHART D

Row numbers: 4, 3, 2, 1

→ 7 patt sts ←

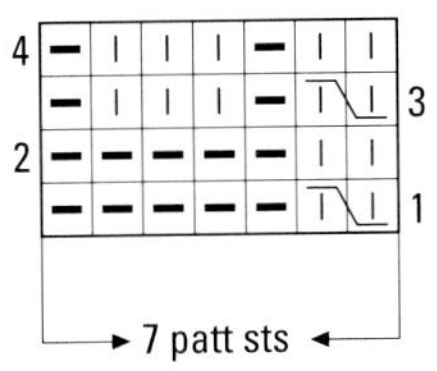

Next Row (WS) – Inc

Patt 14[21,28] as set; m1; * (p2,m1) twice; p1; m1; (p2,m1) twice; p4; (m1,p3) 6 times; m1; p3; rep from * 4 times in all (23[30,37] sts rem on left needle); m1; (p2,m1) twice; p1; m1; (p2,m1) twice; patt 14[21,28] sts as set. 228[242,256] sts.

Change to 3mm (US 3) needles. Beg at row 1 of all charts and set the patt as follows—

Row 1 (RS): Reading all charts from right to left, work chart B over the first 14[21,28] sts, repeating the 7 patt sts 2[3,4] times; work Chart C over the next 200 sts, repeating the 46 patt sts 4 times, then patt the first 16 sts of chart once more; work Chart D over the last 14[21,28] sts, repeating the 7 patt sts 2[3,4] times.

Row 2 (WS): Reading all charts from left to right, work Chart D over the first 14[21,28] sts, repeating the 7 patt sts 2[3,4] times; patt the last 16 sts of chart C, then rep the 46 patt sts 4 times; work Chart B over the last 14[21,28] sts, repeating the 7 patt sts 2[3,4] times. ***

Continue as set and rep all rows of each chart, until front measures 58[61,64]cm from cast on edge, with RS facing for next row .

Shape Front Neck

Patt 97[102,107] sts as set; place the next 34[38,42] sts on a holder for front neck; leave the rem sts on a spare needle.
Turn, and keeping continuity of patt as far as possible throughout, shape left side of neck as follows—
+ Dec 1 st at neck edge of next 6 rows. Patt 1 row without shaping, then dec 1 st at neck edge of next and every foll alt row 9 times in all. 82[87,92] sts rem. Patt 1 row without shaping.
Cast off the rem sts, and during cast off, dec 1 st over each Chart B cable, dec 5 sts evenly over each Chart C 12st cable, and dec 6 sts evenly over Chart C diamond. ++
With RS facing, rejoin yarn to sts of right side, and keeping continuity, patt to end of row.
turn, and keeping continuity of patt, shape neck as left side from + to ++, decreasing over chart D instead of Chart B cables during cast off.

BACK

As front from ** to ***. Continue in patt as set and rep all rows of each chart until back matches front in length at shoulder cast off, with RS facing for next row.
Cast off the first 82[87,92] sts, decreasing during cast off as left front shoulder; patt the next 64[68,72] sts and place these sts on a holder for back neck; cast off the rem 82[87,92] sts, decreasing during cast off as right front shoulder.

SLEEVES

With 2.75mm (US 2) needles, cast on 68 sts. Beg at row 1 of Chart A and set the patt as follows—
Row 1 (RS): Reading from right to left, rep the 7 patt sts 9 times; patt the last 5 sts as indicated.
Row 2 (WS): Reading from left to right, patt the first 5 sts as indicated; rep the 7 patt sts 9 times.
Continue as set and rep the 2 patt rows until cuff measures 6cm, with WS facing for next row.

Next Row (WS) – Inc

Patt 9[5,1]; * m1, p2; rep from * to the last 9[5,1] sts; m1; patt 9[5,1]. 94[98,102] sts.
Change to 3mm (US 3) needles. Beg at row 1 of all charts and set the patt as follows—
Row 1 (RS): Reading from right to left, patt the last 0[2,4] sts of Chart B, then work the 7 patt sts; beg at 15th st and patt the last 32 sts of chart C, then work the 46 patt sts, then work the first 2 sts of rep; work the 7 patt sts of Chart D, then patt the first 0[2,4] sts of rep.
Row 2 (WS): Reading from left to right, patt the last 0[2,4] sts of chart D, then work the 7 patt sts; patt the last 2 sts of Chart C, then work the 46 patt sts, then patt the first 32 sts; work the 7 patt sts of chart B, then patt the first 0[2,4] sts.
Continue in patt as set and inc 1 st at each end of 3rd and every foll 3rd row, working all inc sts into Charts B and D patts, until there are 110[122,134] sts. Then continue as set and inc on every foll 4th row until there are 180[188,196] sts (50[54,58] Charts B and D sts at each side of sleeve). Continue in patt without further shaping until sleeve measures 45[46,47]cm from cast on edge, with RS facing for next row.

Shape Saddle

Cast off 81[85,89] sts at beg of next 2 rows, and during cast off, dec 1 st over each Chart B and D cables, 5 sts evenly over Chart C cables, and 6 sts evenly over Chart C diamonds. 18 centre sleeve sts rem.
P the first and last st on RS rows and k these sts on WS rows and continue working patt as set over the centre 16 sts, until saddle fits in length along shoulder cast off edges of back and front. Place sts on a holder.

FINISHING

Do not press. Block out pieces, right side up, to measurements shown on schematic. Cover with well-dampened towels and leave to dry thoroughly. Alternatively, sew up and complete garment as given below, then rinse in lukewarm water, spin and block out on a woolly board.
Sew saddles along shoulder cast off edges of back and front. Sew cast off edge of sleeves to back and front. Press seams very lightly on WS, using a warm iron and damp cloth, and avoid pressing on cables. Sew up side and sleeve seams as before, omitting Chart A ribs.

Neckband

With RS facing and 3mm (US 3) needles, beg at back neck and pick up and k the 64[68,72] sts from holder, decreasing 4[5,6] sts evenly over centre back cable – 60[63,66] sts rem from holder; pick up and k the 18 sts from left saddle, decreasing 5 sts evenly over cable – 13 sts rem from saddle; knit up 23 sts evenly along left side of neck; pick up the 34[38,42] sts from front neck holder, decreasing 5 sts evenly over centre front cable – 29[33,37] sts rem from holder; knit up 23 sts evenly along right side of neck; pick up and dec right saddle to 13 sts as left, to complete the rnd. 161[168,175] sts.
Place a marker at beg of rnd, and reading both rows of chart from right to left (all rnds are RS), beg at row 1 of Chart A and rep the 7 patt sts 23[24,25] times in the rnd. Work 26[28,30] rnds in total.
Cast off all sts knitwise, decreasing 1 st over each cable during cast off. Darn in loose ends.

Fort Ross

DESIGNED BY JADE STARMORE

SIZES

To fit bust 81-89[91-99,102-112]cm 32-35[36-39,40-44]in. Directions for larger sizes are given in square brackets. Where there is only one set of figures, it applies to all sizes.

KNITTED MEASUREMENTS

Underarm (buttoned) 117[123,129]cm 46[48.5,51]in.
Length 57.5[62,66]cm.
Sleeve length 43cm.

MATERIALS

Of **Scottish Heather**—
6[7,7] Skeins in Brass: 5 skeins in Duck Egg: 4 skeins each in Lacquer and Aster: 2 Skeins each in Burnt Umber and Raspberry. 1 Pair of 4.5mm (US 7) needles. 8 Buttons.

STITCHES

Check Patt : K2 with first colour, k2 with second colour, stranding the yarns evenly across the WS on every row.
Chart Patts: Worked entirely in st.st. (k RS rows, p WS rows). Odd numbered rows are RS and are worked from right to left. Even numbered rows are WS and are worked from left to right. Use separate lengths of yarn for each area of colour. Link one colour to the next on every row by crossing the yarn from the last colour worked **over** the yarn for the next colour before working the next st.

TENSION

19 Sts and 24 rows to 10cm, measured over Chart Patt, using 4.5mm (US 7) needles.

BACK

With 4.5mm (US 7) needles and Brass, cast on 114[122,126] sts. Joining in and breaking off colours as required, work check patt as follows—
Row 1 (RS): * K2 Brass, k2 Duck Egg; rep from * to the last 2 sts; k2 Brass.
Row 2 (WS): As row 1, stranding the yarn on the WS.
Rows 3 & 4: * K2 Lacquer, k2 Brass; rep from * to the last 2 sts; k2 Lacquer.
Rows 5 & 6: * K2 Brass, k2 Aster; rep from * to the last 2 sts; k2 Brass.
Next Row (RS) – Dec
First and Second Sizes: With Brass, k8[4]; (k2tog, k 14[12]) 6[8] times; k2tog; k 8[4]. 107[113] sts.
Third Size: With Brass, k14; (k2tog, k14) 7 times. 119 sts.
All Sizes
With Brass, k 1 row. Using separate lengths of yarn for each area of colour, beg at row 1 of charts and set the patt as follows—
Row 1 (RS) : Reading from right to left, beg on 7th [4th, first] st of chart A as indicated, and patt the 54[57,60] sts (the last st of chart A is the centre back st); then beg at second st of chart B and patt the 53[56,59] sts as indicated.
Row 2 (WS): Reading from left to right, beg at 7th[4th, first]

st of chart B and patt the 53[56,59] sts as indicated; patt the 54[57,60] sts of chart A as indicated.
Continue as set and rep the 60 patt rows twice, then work through row 2[12,22] of charts, thus ending with RS facing for next row.
Shape Back Neck
With colours as for next row of chart, patt the first 40[43,46] sts; leave the rem sts on a spare needle. Keeping continuity of patt throughout, turn and shape left side of neck as follows—
+ Dec 1 st at neck edge of next 2 rows. Patt 1 row without shaping, then dec 1 st at neck edge of next and foll alt row. 36[39,42] sts rem. Patt 1 row without shaping, thus working through row 10[20,30] of charts. Cast off sts. ++
With RS facing, cast off the centre back 27 sts from spare needle, then keeping continuity, patt the rem 40[43,46] sts. Shape right side of neck as left, from + to ++.

RIGHT FRONT

With 4.5mm (US 7) needles and Brass cast on 58[62,64] sts. Work 6 rows of check patt as back (on third size, omit the last 2 sts on RS rows and the first 2 sts on WS rows).
Next Row (RS) – Dec
With Brass, k4[2,7]; * k2tog, k14[12,14]; rep from * to the last 6[4,9] sts; k2tog; k4[2,7]. 54[57,60] sts. With Brass, k 1 row.
Using separate lengths of yarn for each area of colour, beg at row 1 of chart B and set the patt as follows—
Row 1 (RS): Reading from right to left, beg at first st and patt the 54[57,60] sts as indicated.
Row 2 (WS): Reading from left to right, beg at 7th[4th,first] st and patt the 54[57,60] sts as indicated.
Continue as set and work the 60 rows of chart B, then work through row 28[38,48] once more, thus ending with RS facing for next row. Place a marker at beg of row.
Shape Front Neck
Keeping continuity of patt throughout, dec 1 st at beg of next and every foll alt row 12 times in all. 42[45,48] sts rem. Then continue to dec 1 st at same edge of every foll 3rd row, 6 times in all. 36[39,42] sts rem. Patt 1 row without shaping, thus ending on row 10[20,30] inclusive. Cast off sts.

LEFT FRONT

As right front, but work patt from chart A as indicated, thus mirror-imaging right front. Shape neck as right front but beg shaping by decreasing at the end of row 29[39,49].

SLEEVES

With 4.5mm (US 7) needles, cast on 48[50,52] sts. Work 6 rows of check patt as back, (omitting last 2 sts on RS rows and first 2 sts on WS rows on first and third sizes).
Next Row (RS): With Brass, k and dec 1 st at centre of row. 47[49,51] sts. With Brass k 1 row.
Using separate lengths of yarn for each area of colour, beg at row 1 of charts and set the patt as follows—
Row 1 (RS): Reading from right to left, beg at st indicated on chart A and patt the last 24[25,26] sts (the last st is the centre st of sleeve); beg at second st of chart B and patt the

23[24,25] sts as indicated.

Row 2 (WS): Reading from left to right, beg at st indicated on chart B and patt the 23[24,25] sts; patt the first 24[25,26] sts of chart A as indicated.

Continue as set and inc 1 st at each end of 3rd and every foll 4th row, working all inc sts into patt, until there are 95[97,99] sts.

Work through row 35 of charts. 95 Chart patt rows in total. Cast off purlwise on the WS.

FINISHING

Darn in loose ends. Block pieces to measurements shown on schematic. Place markers at each side of back and fronts 25[25.5,26]cm down from shoulder cast off. Sew back and fronts together at shoulder seams. Press seams lightly on WS, using a warm iron and damp cloth.

Right Sleeve Edging

With RS facing, 4.5mm (US 7) needles and Brass, beg at right back marker and knit up 98[102,106] sts evenly to right front marker, working into inside loop of edge st. With Brass, k 1 row.

Join in Duck Egg and work check patt as follows—

Row 1 (RS): * K2 Brass, K2 Duck Egg; rep from * to the last 2 sts; k2 Brass.

Row 2 (WS): As row 1, stranding the yarn on the WS.

Row 3: With Brass, k.

With Brass, cast off knitwise.

Left Sleeve Edging

As right, but beg at left front and knit up sts evenly to left back marker.

Place centre top of sleeves at shoulder seams and sew sleeves to outside loop of body edge st, so that edging overlaps sleeve on the RS. Press seams very lightly on the WS. Sew up side and sleeve seams and press seams lightly on the WS.

Collar

With 4.5mm (US 7) needles and Brass, cast on 267 sts. Joining in and breaking of colours as required, and stranding yarns on WS, work check patt as follows—

Row 1 (RS): (K2 Duck Egg, k2 Brass) 17 times; k2 Duck Egg; k1 Brass and mark this st (right shoulder); * (k2 Duck Egg, k2 Brass) 15 times; k2 Duck Egg; k1 Brass and mark this st (centre back); rep from * once more, thus marking left shoulder st; (k2 Duck Egg, k2 Brass) 17 times; k2 Duck Egg.

Row 2 (WS): With Duck Egg k2tog; (k2 Brass, k2 Duck Egg) 17 times; with Brass p marked st; * (k2 Duck Egg, k2 Brass) 15 times; k2 Duck Egg; with Brass, p marked st; rep from * once more; (k2 Duck Egg, k2 Brass) 17 times; with Duck Egg k2tog.

Row 3: K1 Brass; (k2 Lacquer, k2 Brass) 16 times; k2 Lacquer; k1 Brass; with Brass sl2tog knitwise–k1–p2sso; * k1 Brass; (k2 Lacquer, k2 Brass) 14 times; k2 Lacquer; k1 Brass; with Brass sl2tog knitwise–k1–p2sso; rep from * once more; k1 Brass; (k2 Lacquer, k2 Brass) 16 times; k2 Lacquer; k1 Brass.

Row 4: With Lacquer, k2tog; k1 Lacquer; (k2 Brass, k2 Lacquer) 16 times; sl2tog purlwise tbl–p1–p2sso; (k2 Lacquer, k2 Brass) 14 times; k2 Lacquer; k1 Brass; p1 Brass; k1 Brass; (k2 Lacquer, k2 Brass) 14 times; k2 Lacquer; sl2tog purlwise tbl–p1–p2sso; (k2 Lacquer, k2 Brass) 16 times; k1 Lacquer;

with Lacquer k2tog.

Row 5: (K2 Aster, k2 Brass) 16 times; k1 Brass; with Brass sl2tog knitwise–k1–p2sso; k1 Brass; (k2 Aster, k2 Brass) 14 times; with Brass sl2tog knitwise–k1–p2sso; (k2 Brass, k2 Aster) 14 times; k1 Brass; with Brass sl2tog knitwise–k1–p2sso; k1 Brass; (k2 Aster, k2 Brass) 16 times.

Row 6: With Brass k2tog; (k2 Aster, k2 Brass) 15 times; k2 Aster; with Brass sl2tog purlwise tbl–p1–p2sso; (k2 Aster, k2 Brass) 14 times; p1 Brass; (k2 Brass, k2 Aster) 14 times; with Brass sl2tog purlwise–p1–p2sso; (k2 Aster, k2 Brass) 15 times, with Brass, k2tog.

Continue working check patt in colour sequence as set and work shoulder decreases in Brass on every row, and work centre back decrease in Brass on every RS row (purl the centre back st in Brass on WS rows) as set. AT THE SAME TIME keep continuity of check patt and cast off 2 sts at beg of next 2 rows; 4 sts at beg of next 2 rows; 6 sts at beg of next 12 rows.

Next Row (RS): With Brass cast off 27 sts; keeping continuity patt to end of row without decreasing at centre back or left shoulder.

Next Row (WS): With Brass, cast off 27 sts, patt the rem centre 25 sts without decreasing at centre back.

Turn and with Brass, cast off sts.

Left Front Band

With RS facing, 4.5mm (US 7) needles and Brass, beg at neck shaping marker and knit up 76[80,84] sts evenly along right front edge to cast on edge. With Brass k 1 row. Joining in and breaking off colours as required, and stranding yarn on WS, work check patt as follows—

Row 1 (RS): With Brass k2tog; * k2 Aster, k2 Brass; rep from * to the last 2 sts; k2 Aster.

Row 2 (WS): * K2 Aster, k2 Brass; rep from * to the last st; k1 Brass.

Row 3: With Brass k2tog; k1 Brass; * k2 Lacquer, k2 Brass; rep from * to end of row.

Row 4: * K2 Brass, k2 Lacquer; rep from * to the last 2 sts; k2 Brass.

Row 5: With Duck Egg k2tog; * k2 Brass, k2 Duck Egg; rep from * to end of row.

Row 6: * K2 Duck Egg, k2 Brass; rep from * to the last st; k1 Duck Egg.

Next row: With Brass k2tog; k to end of row.

With Brass, cast off knitwise.

Right Front Band

As right but beg at cast on edge and knit up sts evenly to neck shaping marker. Shape top of band as right band, but decreasing at the end of RS rows.

Pin centre back of RS of collar to WS of centre back neck and pin and sew collar to neck and top of front edgings. Fold collar to RS and press fold line very gently on WS.

Button Loops

Using 1 strand each of Aster, Lacquer and Duck Egg make 8 plaits each 10 cm long and knot and trim ends. Fold each plait in half to make loops and sew together leaving an opening of 25mm in diameter. Sew 5 loops to right front band, placing them adjacent to centre of pattern crosses. Sew a loop at centre back and shoulders of collar. Sew buttons to left front at centre pattern crosses, and to shoulders and centre back.

CHART A

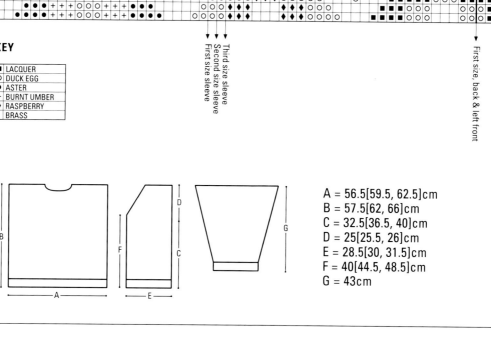

KEY

■	LACQUER
○	DUCK EGG
●	ASTER
+	BURNT UMBER
◆	RASPBERRY
	BRASS

Third size sleeve
Second size sleeve
First size sleeve

First size, back & left front
Second size, back & left front
Third size, back & left front

A = 56.5[59.5, 62.5]cm
B = 57.5[62, 66]cm
C = 32.5[36.5, 40]cm
D = 25[25.5, 26]cm
E = 28.5[30, 31.5]cm
F = 40[44.5, 48.5]cm
G = 43cm

CHART B

Third size, back & right front
Second size, back & right front
First size, back & right front
First size sleeve
Second size sleeve
Third size sleeve
All sizes right front
All sizes back & sleeve

DRAWINGS 1A, B & C: Sl2tog knitwise–k1–p2sso

DRAWING 1A: insert the right needle point through the next two stitches, from front to back (knitwise) as shown: then slip the two stitches together to the right needle.

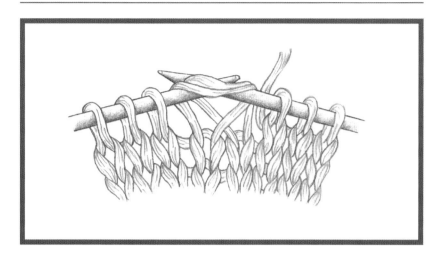

DRAWING 1B: knit the next stitch on the left needle (k1).

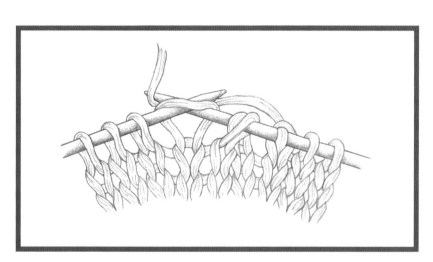

DRAWING 1C: pass the two slipped stitches over the knit stitch and drop them off the needle (p2sso). The centre stitch of the group sits vertically in front of the two eliminated stitches.

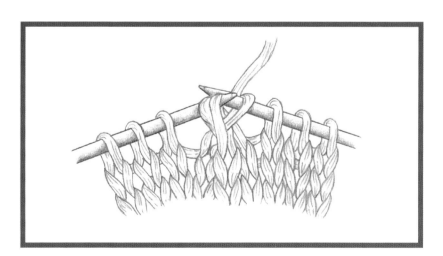

The collar is shaped at the shoulders and centre back by working vertical double decreases which eliminates two stitches on every row at the shoulders, and on every right side row at the centre back. Drawings 1A, B & C show how to work the decrease on right side rows (sl2tog knitwise–k1–p2sso). Drawings 2A, B & C show how to work the same decrease on wrong side rows (sl2tog purlwise tbl–p1–p2sso).

DRAWINGS 2A, B & C: Sl2tog purlwise tbl–p1–p2sso

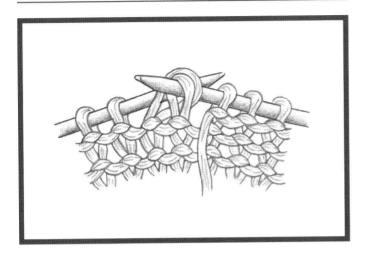

DRAWING 2A: insert the right needle point, from back to front (purlwise), through the back loops (tbl) of the next two stitches, and slip the stitches together to the right needle.

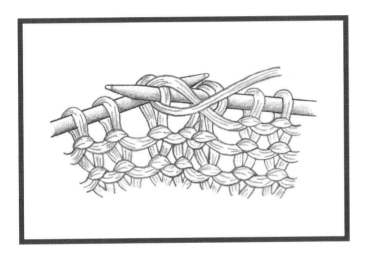

DRAWING 2B: purl the next st on the left needle (p1).

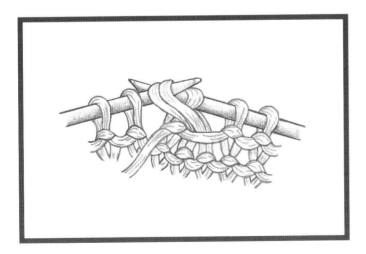

DRAWING 2C: pass the two slipped stitches over the purl stitch and drop them off the needle (p2sso).

Russian River

SIZES

To fit chest/bust 86-97[102-112]cm 34-38[40-44]in.
Directions for larger size are given in square brackets. Where there is only one set of figures, it applies to both sizes.

KNITTED MEASUREMENTS

Underarm 118.5[128]cm 46.5[50.5]in.
Length 66[70]cm.
Sleeve length 44cm.

MATERIALS

Of **Scottish Campion** —
4 Skeins each of Sphagnum and Bracken.
3 Skeins each of Cerise and Marjoram.
2 Skeins each of Oasis, Madder, Brick, Flamingo, Carmine.
1 Skein each of Cranberry and Terra Cotta.
1 Set of double-pointed or circular 3.25mm (US 3) needles.
1 Set of Double-pointed 2.75mm (US 2) needles.
2 Stitch holders. 2 Safety pins. Stitch markers.

STITCHES

2/2 Rib: K2 with first colour, p2 with second colour, stranding the yarns evenly across the WS. **Chart Patt:** All rnds are read from right to left. K every rnd stranding the yarn not in immediate use evenly across the WS. **Steeks:** Worked at armholes and front and back neck, and later cut up centre to form openings. Each steek is worked over 8 sts and k in alt colours on every st and rnd. Do not weave in newly joined in or broken off yarns at centre of first armhole steek. Instead leave approx 5cm tail when joining in and breaking off yarns. **Edge St:** Worked at each side of steeks and k in background colours throughout. Sts for sleeves and neckband are knitted up from edge st. **Cross Stitch:** With darning needle, overcast trimmed steeks to strands on WS, and after sewing to end, reverse to form cross stitches.

TENSION

30 Sts and 34 rows to 10cm, measured over chart patt using 3.25mm (US 3) needles. To make an accurate tension swatch, cast on 34 sts on 1 double-pointed or circular needle and work the 34 sts shown on chart, **knitting on the RS only,** breaking off the yarns at the end of every row. Read all rows from right to left and beg at row 1, work 36 rows.

BODY

With 3.25mm (US 3) needles and Sphagnum, cast on 336[364] sts. Place a marker at beg of rnd, and making sure cast on edge is not twisted, join in and break off colours as required and work 2/2 rib as follows—
Rnd 1: * K2 Terra Cotta, p2 Sphagnum; rep from * to end of rnd.
Rnd 2; * K2 Flamingo; p2 Sphagnum; rep from * to end of rnd.

Rnd 3: * K2 Flamingo, p2 Bracken; rep from * to end of rnd.
Rnd 4: * K2 Brick, p2 Bracken; rep from * to end of rnd.
Rnd 5: * K2 Brick, p2 Marjoram; rep from * to end of rnd.
Rnds 6, 7 & 8: * K2 Madder, p2 Marjoram; rep from * to end of rnd.
Rnd 9: As rnd 5.
Rnd 10: As rnd 4.
Rnd 11: As rnd 3.
Rnd 12: As rnd 2.
Rnds 13 & 14: As rnd 1.
Rnd 15: * K2 Cerise, p2 Sphagnum; rep from * to end of rnd.
Rnd 16: * K2 Cerise, p2 Bracken; rep from 8 to end of rnd.
Rnd 17: * K2 Carmine, p2 Bracken; rep from * to end of rnd.
Rnd 18: * K2 Carmine, p2 Oasis; rep from * to end of rnd.
Rnd 19: * K2 Cranberry, p2 Oasis; rep from * to end of rnd.
Rnd 20: As rnd 18.
Rnd 21: As rnd 17.
Rnd 22: As rnd 16.
Rnd 23: As rnd 15.
Rnd 24: As rnd 1.
Next Rnd – Inc
With Sphagnum, (m1, k17[18]) 4 times; (m1, k16[19]) twice; (m1, k 17[18]) 8 times; (m1, k16[19]) twice; (m1, k17[18]) 4 times. 356[384] sts.
Place a marker at beg of rnd, and joining in and breaking of colours as required, beg at rnd 1 of chart and reading all rnds from right to left, set the patt as follows—
First Size: * Patt the first 5 sts as indicated; rep the 24 patt sts 7 times; patt the last 5 sts as indicated; rep from * once more to complete the rnd.
Second Size: Rep the 24 patt sts 16 times in the rnd.
Both Sizes: Continue as set and rep the 24 patt rnds and work 121[130] chart patt rnds in total, thus ending on rnd 1[10] inclusive. Break off yarns.
Next Rnd – Work Armhole Steeks and Edge Sts
Place the first st of rnd on a safety pin; with alt colours as for rnd 2[11] of chart cast on 4 steek sts and mark the first st cast on for beg of rnd; with background colour cast on 1 edge st; keeping continuity, patt the next 177[191] sts (front); place the next st on a safety pin; with background colour cast on 1 edge st; with alt colours, cast on 8 steek sts; with background colour cast on 1 edge st; keeping continuity, patt the next 177[191] sts (back); with background colour cast on 1 edge st; with alt colours cast on 4 steek sts.
Work steek sts in alt colours and edge sts in background colours throughout and continue working chart patt over the front and back sts until 180[190] chart patt rnds have been worked in total, thus ending on rnd 12[22] inclusive.
Next Rnd – Work Front Neck Steek and Edge Sts
With alt colours as for rnd 13[23] of chart k4 steek sts; k1 edge st; keeping continuity, patt the first 73[79] sts of front; place the next 31[33] sts on a holder; cast on 10 steek and edge sts (first and last sts cast on are edge sts, centre 8 are steek sts); keeping continuity, patt the rem 73[79] sts of front and work straight as set to end of rnd.
Work front neck steek and edge sts as armholes, and keeping continuity of patt, dec 1 st at chart patt side of front neck edge sts on next 4 rnds. Patt 1 rnd without shaping

CHART

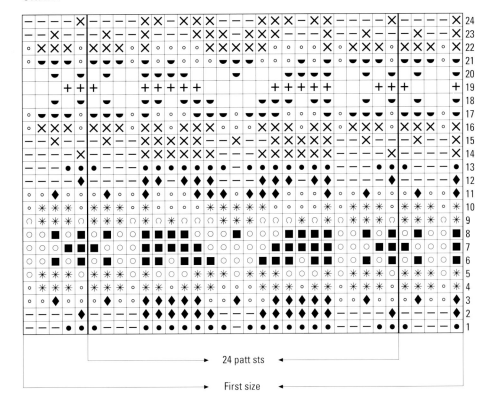

24 patt sts

First size

KEY

—	SPHAGNUM
●	TERRA COTTA
♦	FLAMINGO
∘	BRACKEN
✳	BRICK
○	MARJORAM
■	MADDER
✕	CERISE
◡	CARMINE
+	CRANBERRY
	OASIS

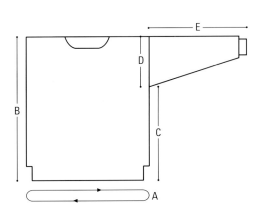

A = 118.5[128]cm
B = 66[70]cm
C = 42[45]cm
D = 24[25]cm
E = 44cm

then dec as set on next and every foll alt rnd until 64[69] chart patt sts rem on each front shoulder.

Next Rnd – Work Back Neck Steek and Edge Sts

Keeping continuity, patt straight as set to the 177[191] sts of back; Patt the first 64[69] sts of back; place the next 49[53] sts on a holder; cast on 10 steek and edge sts as front neck; keeping continuity, patt the rem 64[69] sts of back and work straight as set to end of rnd.

Continue as set and dec 1 st at chart patt side of front and back neck edge sts on next and foll 2 alt rnds. 61[66] chart patt sts rem on each shoulder. Patt 3 rnds without shaping and cast off all steek sts on the last rnd.

With Sphagnum, graft back and front shoulder sts together, including edge sts.

SLEEVES

Cut open armhole steeks up centre, between 4th and 5th steek sts. With 3.25mm (US 3) needles and Marjoram pick up and k the st from safety pin and mark this st for beg of rnd and underarm st; knit up 145[151] sts evenly around armhole, working into loop of edge st next to chart patt sts. 146[152] sts. Turn chart upside down and joining in and breaking off colours as required, beg at rnd 9 and set the patt as follows—

With Marjoram k the underarm st; reading from right to left in upside down position, patt the last 1[4] sts of 24 st rep; rep the 24 patt sts 6 times; patt the first 0[3] sts of 24 st rep. Working the underarm st in background colours throughout, work back through the chart rnds and patt the next 3 rnds as set.

Next Rnd – Beg Sleeve Shaping

With colours as for next rnd of chart, k the underarm st; with background colour k2tog; keeping continuity, patt as set to the last 2 sts; with background colour ssk.

Keeping continuity, patt back through the next 3 rnds of chart without shaping.

Rep these last 4 rnds until 98[110] sts rem. Then continue and dec as set on every foll 3rd rnd until 76[80] sts rem, thus working 129 chart patt rnds in total and ending on rnd 1 inclusive.

Next Rnd – Dec for Cuff

First Size: With Sphagnum, k4; * k2tog, k4; rep from * to end of rnd. 64 sts.

Second Size: With Sphagnum, K6; * k2tog, k4; rep from * to the last 8 sts; k2tog, k6. 68 sts.

Both Sizes: Change to double-pointed 2.75mm (US 2) needles, and joining in and breaking off colours as required, work 24 rnds of 2/2 rib as body, but working colour sequence from rnd 24 back through to rnd 1. With Sphagnum, cast off knitwise.

Neckband

Cut open front and back neck steeks up centre, between 4th and 5th steek sts.

With 3.25mm (US 3) needles and Sphagnum, beg at back neck and pick up and k the 49[53] sts from holder; knit up 26[27] sts evenly along left side of neck, working into loop of edge st next to chart patt sts; pick up and k the 31[33] sts from front neck holder; knit up 26[27] sts evenly along right side of neck, working as left, to complete the rnd. 132[140] sts.

Place a marker at beg of rnd and work 24 rnds of 2/2 rib in colour sequence as cuffs. With Sphagnum, cast off knitwise.

FINISHING

Trim all steeks to a 2st width and with Sphagnum, cross st steeks in position. Using a warm iron and damp cloth, press garment on the WS, omitting ribs.

Sand Dollar

DESIGNED BY JADE STARMORE

To fit bust 81-86[89-97,99-107]cm 32-34[35-38,39-42]in. Directions for larger sizes are given in square brackets. Where there is only one set of figures, it applies to all sizes.

KNITTED MEASUREMENTS

Underarm (ex. gussets) 90[100,112]cm 35.5[39.5,44]in.
Length 76[80,85]cm.
Sleeve length 43[43.5,44]cm.

MATERIALS

14[15,16] balls of **Scottish Fleet** shown in Pink and Cream.
1 Set of double-pointed or circular 3mm (US 3) needles.
Note: If you use circular needles, you will also require 2 double-pointed 3mm needles to work the shoulder join.
1 Set of double-pointed or short circular 2.75mm (US 2) needles.
1 Cable needle. 6 Stitch holders. Stitch markers.

STITCHES

Chart Patts: On areas worked in the round, all charts are read from right to left. On areas worked back and forth in rows, all RS rows are read from right to left and all WS rows are worked from left to right. **Note:** On charts A through F, all make ones' (M) are worked by picking up the strand running between the last stitch worked and the next st to be worked, and knitting into the back of the strand. On underarm gussets, all make ones' (M) are worked by picking up the loop of the stitch **below** the next st to be worked and k on RS, or p on WS, into the loop. See pages 70–71.

TENSION

28 Sts and 40 rows to 10cm, measured over chart H patt, using 3mm (US 3) needles. To make a swatch, cast on 40 sts and rep the 10 patt sts 4 times.

BODY

With set of double-pointed or circular 3mm (US 3) needles, cast on 480[540,600] sts. Place a marker at beg of rnd, and making sure cast on edge is not twisted, k1 rnd, then p 1 rnd.
Beg at rnd 1 of chart A and rep the 30 patt sts 16[18,20] times in the rnd. Continue as set and rep the 12 patt rnds of chart A 3[3,4] times in all (36[36,48] rnds).
Work rnd 1 of chart B repeating the 28 patt sts 16[18,20] times in the rnd. 448[504,560] sts rem. Continue as set and work through rnd 12 of chart. Rep the 12 patt rnds 2 more times (36 rnds chart B in total), but on these reps, work M1 instead of first and last k sts on row 1, as indicated on chart, so that the stitch count remains the same throughout all rnds of chart B.
Beg at rnd 1 of chart C repeating the 26 patt sts 16[18,20] times in the rnd. 416[468,520] sts rem. Continue as set and work through rnd 12 of chart. Rep the 12 patt rnds 1[2,2]

KEY

☐ p on RS rows; k on WS rows.

☐ k on RS rows; p on WS rows.

☐ k into back of st on RS rows; p into back of st on WS rows.

☐ k1, p1, k1 into SAME st, thus making 3 sts from 1.

☐ p3tog.

☐ sl 2 sts tog knitwise; k1; pass the 2 slipped sts over the k st.

M make 1 st by picking up the strand between the last st worked and the next st, and k into the back of strand.

☐☐ sl first st to cn and hold at back; k into back of next st; p1 from cn.

☐☐ sl first st to cn and hold at front; p1; k into back of st from cn.

☐☐ sl next st to cn and hold at back; k1b; k1 from cn.

☐☐ sl next st to cn and hold at front; k1; k1b from cn.

☐☐☐ sl first st to cn and hold at back; k2b; p1 from cn.

☐☐☐ sl first 2 sts to cn and hold at front; p1; k2b from cn.

☐ (k1b, k1) into same st, then insert left hand needle point between the vertical strand that runs down between the 2 sts just made and k into this strand, making the third st of the group.

☐ sl 2 sts knitwise, one at a time, with yarn at back, drop yarn, then pass the second st on right needle over first (centre st): sl centre st back to left needle and pass next st on left needle over it: k the rem centre st.

☐☐☐ sl first st to cn and hold at back; k2b; then k1b from cn.

☐☐☐ sl first 2 sts to cn and hold at front; k1b; then k2b from cn.

☐☐☐ sl first 2 sts to cn and hold at front; k1; k2b from cn.

☐☐☐ sl first st to cn and hold at back; k2b; k1 from cn.

☐ no stitch.

CHART A

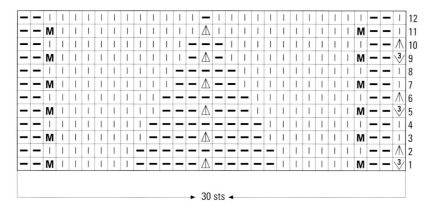

30 sts

CHART B

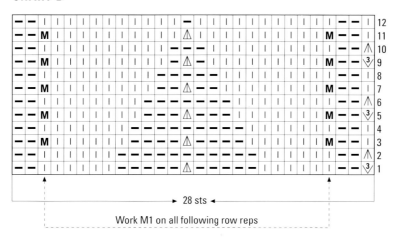

28 sts

Work M1 on all following row reps

CHART C

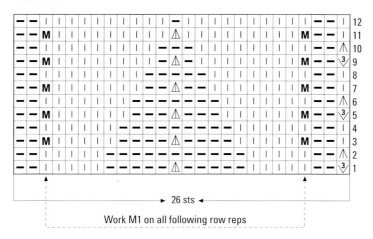

26 sts

Work M1 on all following row reps

CHART D

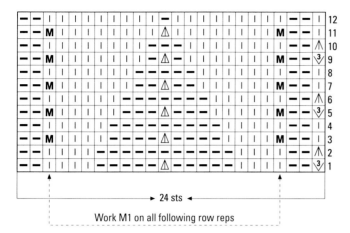

→ 24 sts ←

Work M1 on all following row reps

CHART E

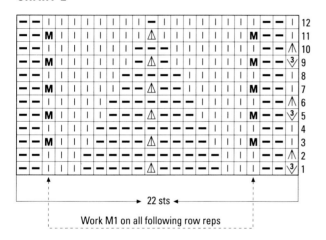

→ 22 sts ←

Work M1 on all following row reps

CHART F

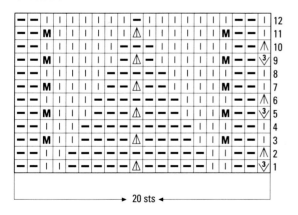

→ 20 sts ←

more times (24[36,36] rnds chart C in total), but on these reps work M1 on row 1, as indicated on chart, thus keeping the st count the same throughout.

Beg at rnd 1 of chart D repeating the 24 patt sts 16[18,20] times in the rnd. 384[432,480] sts rem. Continue as set and work through rnd 12 of chart. Rep the 12 patt rnds once more (24 rnds chart D in total), but on second rep, work M1 on row 1 as indicated on chart, thus keeping the stitch count the same throughout.

Beg at rnd 1 of chart E repeating the 22 patt sts 16[18,20] times in the rnd. 352[396,440] sts rem. Continue as set and work through rnd 12 of chart. Rep the 12 patt rnds once more (24 rnds chart E in total), but on second rep work M1 on row 1 as indicated on chart, thus keeping the stitch count the same throughout.

Beg at rnd 1 of chart F repeating the 20 patt sts 16[18,20] times in the rnd. 320[360,400] sts rem. Continue as set and work though rnd 12 of chart.

Next Rnd – Dec and Mark Gusset Sts

First Size: * K1 and mark this st for gusset; k4; (k2tog, k2) 37 times; k2tog; k5; rep from * once more. 244 sts.

Second Size: * K1 and mark this st for gusset; k2; (k2tog, k2) 16 times; (k2tog, k3) 9 times; (k2tog, k2) 17 times; rep from * once more. 276 sts.

Third Size: * K1 and mark this st for gusset; k2; (k2tog, k2) 16 times; (k2tog, k3) 13 times; (k2tog, k2) 17 times; rep from * once more. 308 sts.

All Sizes – Beg Gussets

Next Rnd: Working all incs into loop below next st, m1; k1; m1 (these 3 sts form the first gusset); p 121[137,153] sts (back); m1; k1; m1 (these 3 sts form the second gusset); p 121[137,153] sts (front).

Next 2 Rnds: * K3 gusset sts; p 121[137,153] sts; rep from * once more.

Next 2 Rnds: K.

Next Rnd – Inc Gussets and Set Chart G Patt

* M1; k3; m1 (gusset); beg at rnd 1 of chart G and patt the first 4 sts as indicated; rep the 8 patt sts (inc as indicated); 14[16,18] times; patt the last 5 sts as indicated. 151[171,191] chart G sts; rep from * once more.

Continue as set, working all gusset sts in k throughout and inc as set at each side of gusset on every foll 4th rnd, and work the 24 rnds of chart G on back and front sts as set, decreasing on back and front on rnd 24 as indicated on chart. 121[137,153] sts rem on each of back and front. Continue to inc as set at each side of gussets on every 4th rnd until there are 19 sts in each gusset, and AT THE SAME TIME, patt the back and front sts as follows—

K on next 2 rnds. P on next 3 rnds. K on next rnd.

Divide for Back and Front Yokes

* K the 19 gusset sts and place these sts on a holder; inc over the next 121[137,153] sts as follows—

k2[2,5]; (m1, k 13[12,11]) 9[11,13] times; m1; k2[3,5]. 131[149,167] sts; rep from * once more. Break off yarn and place the last 131[149,167] sts (front) on a spare needle.

Back Yoke

+ With RS facing and working back and forth in rows, set the yoke patt over the 131[149,167] sts of back as follows—

Row 1 (RS): Reading from right to left, patt the first 4[3,2]

CHART G

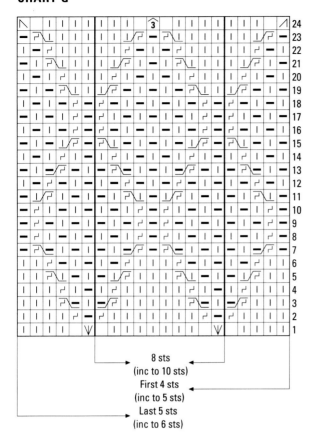

8 sts
(inc to 10 sts)
First 4 sts
(inc to 5 sts)
Last 5 sts
(inc to 6 sts)

CHART H

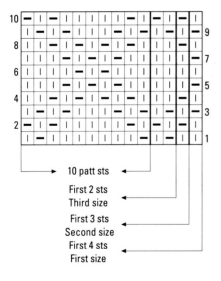

10 patt sts

First 2 sts
Third size
First 3 sts
Second size
First 4 sts
First size

CHART K

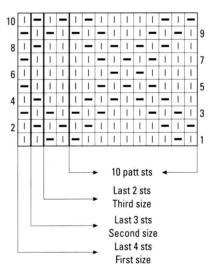

10 patt sts

Last 2 sts
Third size
Last 3 sts
Second size
Last 4 sts
First size

CHART J

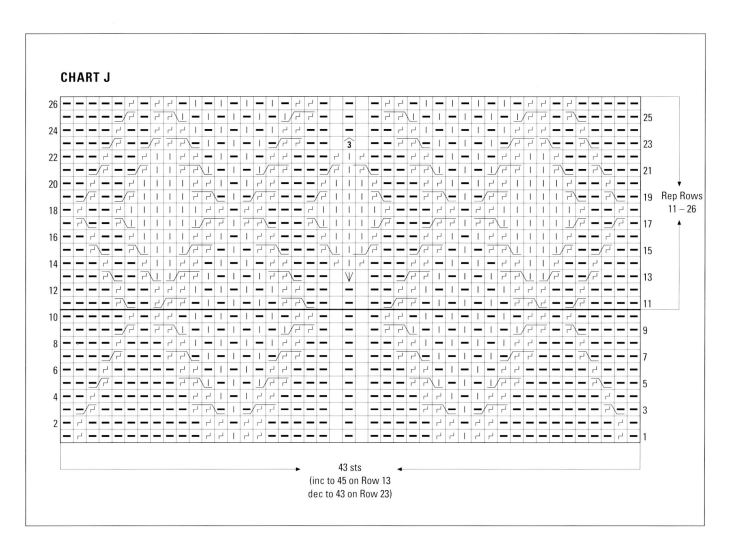

Rep Rows
11 – 26

43 sts
(inc to 45 on Row 13
dec to 43 on Row 23)

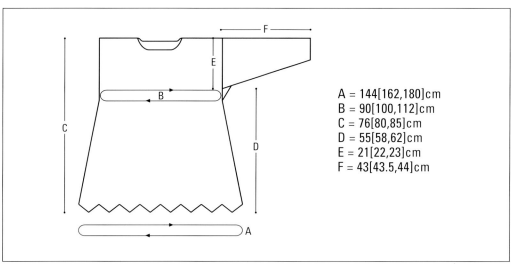

A = 144[162,180]cm
B = 90[100,112]cm
C = 76[80,85]cm
D = 55[58,62]cm
E = 21[22,23]cm
F = 43[43.5,44]cm

sts of chart H as indicated, then rep the 10 patt sts 4[5,6] times; work chart J over the next 43 sts; rep the 10 patt sts of chart K 4[5,6] times, then patt the last 4[3,2] sts as indicated.

Row 2 (WS): Reading from left to right, patt the first 4[3,2] sts of chart K as indicated, then rep the 10 patt sts 4[5,6] times; work chart J over the next 43 sts; rep the 10 patt sts of chart H 4[5,6] times then patt the last 4[3,2] sts as indicated.

Continue as set and rep the 10 patt rows of charts H and K and work through row 10 of chart J once and thereafter, rep rows 11 – 26 (inc 2 sts on row 13 and dec 2 sts on row 23, as indicated).**++**

Work 84[88,92] patt rows in total, thus ending after working row 4[8,2] of charts H and K, and row 20[24,12] of chart J.

Shape Back Neck

Next Row (RS): K 34[42,50] sts; place the next 65[65,67] sts on a holder; leave the rem sts on a spare needle. Turn and shape left shoulder as follows—

Next Row (WS): K2tog; k to end of row. 33[41,49] sts rem. P 2 rows. Place sts on a holder.

With RS facing rejoin yarn to the 34[42,50] sts on spare needle and k to end of row. Shape right shoulder as follows—

Next Row (WS): K to the last 2 sts; k2tog. 33[41,49] sts rem. P 2 rows. Place sts on a holder.

Front Yoke

Work as back yoke from **+** to **++**. Work 66[68,72] patt rows in total, thus ending after working row 6[8,2] of charts H and K, and row 18[20,24] of chart J.

Shape Front Neck

Next Row (RS): Keeping continuity, patt the 44[53,62] sts of chart H; place the 45[45,43] sts of chart J on a holder; leave the rem sts on a spare needle. Turn and shape left side of neck as follows—

+ Keeping continuity of patt, dec 1 st at neck edge of the next 4[4,6] rows, then on every foll alt row 6[7,6] times. 34[42,50] sts rem. Patt 1 row without shaping, thus ending with RS facing for next row. **++**

Next Row: K to the last 2 sts; k2tog. 33[41,49] sts rem. K 1 row. P 2 rows. Place sts on a holder.

With RS facing rejoin yarn to the 44[53,62] sts of right side, and keeping continuity of chart K, patt to end of row. Shape right side as left, from **+** to **++**.

Next Row (RS): K2tog; k to end of row. 33[41,49] sts rem. K 1 row. P 2 rows. Place sts on a holder.

Join Shoulders

Turn body inside out (shoulders are joined on WS). Place front and back sts of one shoulder on two separate double-pointed 3mm (US 3) needles. Hold the needles with shoulder sts parallel, with RS of yokes together, and with a third 3mm (US 3) needle beg at armhole edge and cast off sts together, working to neck edge. Break of yarn and fasten off.

SLEEVES

With RS facing and 3mm (US 3) needles, k the 19 sts from gusset holder; knit up 119[125,131] sts evenly around armhole to complete the rnd.

Shape Gussets and Set Sleeve Patt

Place a marker on right hand needle to mark beg of rnd.

Next Rnd: Ssk; k15; k2tog (gusset); beg at rnd 1 of chart H and patt the last 5[3,1] sts of 10 st rep, then rep the 10 patt sts 11[12,13] times, then patt the first 4[2,0] sts of 10 st rep. Continue working chart H over sleeve sts as set, and working all gusset sts in k throughout, dec 1 st at each side of gusset as set, on every foll 4th rnd until 3 gusset sts rem. Work 3 rnds as set, without shaping.

Next Rnd: Sl1-k2tog-psso (1 gusset st rem); continue in patt as set to end of rnd. 120[126,132] sts.

Next Rnd: P1 and mark this st for seam st and beg of rnd; continue in patt as set to end of rnd.

Next 3 Rnds: P seam st; continue in patt as set to end of rnd.

Next Rnd: P seam st; k2tog; keeping continuity, patt as set to the last 2 sts; ssk.

Rep these last 4 rnds until 56[60,64] sts rem. Continue straight as set until sleeve measures 42[42.5,43]cm from pick-up line.

Next Rnd – Dec

First Size: K2tog; k8; (k2tog, k7) 4 times; k2tog; k8. 50 sts.

Second Size: (K2tog, k8) 6 times. 54 sts.

Third Size: (K2tog, k9) twice; (k2tog, k8) twice; (k2tog, k9) twice. 58 sts.

All Sizes: K 1 rnd. P3 rnds. Cast off purlwise.

Neckband

With RS facing and set of double-pointed or circular 2.75mm (US 2) needles, beg at back neck holder and pick up and k the 65[65,67] sts from holder and dec 6[4,4] sts evenly over chart J patt – 59[61,63] sts rem from holder; knit up 21[22,23] sts sts evenly along left neck edge; pick up and k the 45[45,43] sts from front neck holder and dec 6[6,4] sts evenly – 39 sts rem from holder; knit up 21[22,23] sts evenly along right neck edge to complete the rnd. 140[144,148] sts.

Place a marker at beg of rnd and p 3 rnds. K 1 rnd.

Next Rnd – Dec

K 0[4,8]; * k2tog, k12; rep from * to end of rnd. 130[134,138] sts.

All Sizes: P 3 rnds. K 2 rnds. P 2 rnds. Cast off purlwise.

FINISHING

Rinse in lukewarm water. Spin and lay out garment on towels on a flat surface, away from direct heat/sunlight. Smooth out to measurements given on schematic, using pins to anchor the pointed ends of the hemline. Leave in position to dry completely.

Technical Tip: Sand Dollar Shaping

MAIN BODY PATTERN

The pattern on the main body (charts A–F) is formed by working strategically placed increases and decreases on every alternate round. At each side of the pattern panels, a single increase is worked to form a new stitch, shown on the charts as the symbol **M** (make 1 stitch). The method used to make the increases is shown in DRAWING 1.

The stitch count is maintained by working a double decrease which eliminates two stitches at the centre of each panel. In this case, the centre three stitches are purled together (p3tog) as shown in DRAWING 2.

The pattern panels are gradually reduced to produce the A-line shaping. This is achieved by omitting the increases on the rounds specified in the instructions. This means that the stitches will be reduced on these rounds by twice the number of pattern panels in the garment.

INCREASING THE GUSSETS

The gussets are formed under each armhole by regularly increasing a stitch (m1) at each side of the gusset stitches. The method used in the gussets is known as the *lifted increase,* as shown in DRAWING 3.

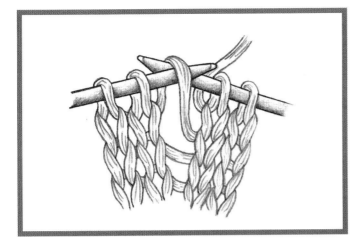

DRAWING 1: M BETWEEN STITCHES

Insert the left needle point, from front to back, under the strand that runs between the two needles: knit into the back of the strand, as shown. The strand will cross at the base when the new stitch is made.

DRAWING 2: PURL 3 TOGETHER (P3TOG)

Insert the right needle through the fronts of the next three stitches, as shown and purl to form one stitch. Note: exert a little more tension on the new stitch to prevent the weight of the three stitches from stretching it.

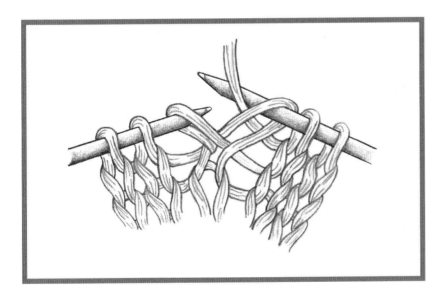

DRAWING 3: LIFTED INCREASE

Insert the right needlepoint through the front of the loop below the next stitch, as shown: then knit into this loop to form the new stitch.

Point Reyes

DESIGNED BY JADE STARMORE

KNITTED MEASUREMENTS

Width 68cm 26.75in.
Length 90cm 35.5in.

MATERIALS

Of **Scottish Campion**—
3 Skeins of Cobalt.
2 Skeins each of Pale Turquoise, Scotch Broom and Rye.
1 Skein each of Turquoise, Crimson, Campbell Red, Pumpkin, Seabright, Cream and Forget-Me-Not.
1 Set of double-pointed or circular 3.25mm (US 3) needles.
1 100cm long circular 3.25mm needle. **Note:** The edging is worked in the round, beginning with a total of 852 sts and ending with a total of 932 sts. A long circular needle will ensure that this can be comfortably worked in one piece. Stitch markers.

STITCHES

Chart Patt: All rnds are read from right to left. K every rnd, stranding the yarn not in immediate use evenly across the WS. On rnds where there are more than 8 sts in one colour, weave in the stranded yarn once at the centre of the group. **Steek:** Worked up chart patt length and later cut up centre to form a flat piece. The steek is worked over 8 sts and k on every rnd. On two-colour rnds, the steek sts are worked in alt colours on every st and rnd. Join in and break off colours as they are used, at centre of steek – this is also the beg of the rnd. Do not weave in newly joined in or broken off yarns at the centre of the steek, Instead leave approx. 5cm tail when joining in and breaking off yarns. **Edge Stitch:** Worked at each side of steek and k in background colours throughout. Sts for side edgings are knitted up from edge sts. **Check Patt:** Worked on edging. K2 with first colour, k2 with second colour, stranding the yarns evenly across the WS. The next and every alt rnd is worked in p. It is important to remember to strand the yarn on the WS after every p2. **Note:** Take care not to strand the yarn too tightly across the WS, especially near the corners of the edging where the stitches are grouped closely together on the needle. The tension of the check stitch should remain the same as that of the chart patt.

TENSION

30 Sts and 34 rows to 10cm, measured over chart patt using 3.25mm (US 3) needles. To make an accurate tension swatch, cast on 37 sts on 1 double-pointed or circular needle and work a flat piece, **knitting on the RS only**, breaking off the yarn at the end of every row.

BABY BLANKET

With 3.25mm (US 3) needles and Cream, cast on 191 sts. Place a marker at beg of rnd, and making sure cast on edge is not twisted, k 1 rnd.
Next Rnd: Cast off the first 5 sts; k 181 sts; cast off the last 5 sts. Break off Cream.
Next Rnd: With Cobalt, cast on 5 sts and mark the first st cast on for beg of rnd; k 181 sts; cast on 5 sts. 191 sts.
Join in Scotch Broom and beg at rnd 2 of chart, set the steek, edge sts and patt as follows—
With alt colours, k4 steek sts; with Cobalt k1 edge st; reading from right to left, rep the 36 patt sts 5 times; patt the last st as indicated; with Cobalt k1 edge st; with alt colours, k4 steek sts.
Joining in and breaking off colours as required, continue as set, working the edge sts in background colours throughout, and the steek sts in alt colours on two-colour rnds. Rep the 63 patt rnds 4 times in all, then work through rnd 27 once more, casting off the steek and edge sts on the 27th rnd. 181 sts rem and 279 chart patt rnds worked in total. Leave sts on needle.

Edging

Cut open steek up centre between 4th and 5th steek sts. Unpick Cream cast on and k rows, and place the 181 loops of first Cobalt row on a spare needle.
With 100cm long 3.25mm (US 3) circular needle, RS facing and Cobalt, beg at top left corner and working into loop of edge st next to chart patt, knit up 245 sts along the rows of left side as follows—
Knit up 15 sts into first 15 rows; * miss 1 row; knit up 7 sts into next 7 rows; rep from * to bottom edge – 245 sts; place a marker on the last st knit up; k the 181 loops of bottom edge and place a marker on the last st; knit up 245 sts along right side, working as left, and place a marker on the last st knit up; k the 181 sts of top edge and place a marker on the last st. 852 sts. There are now markers at each of the 4 corners, with beg of rnd at top left side.
Next Rnd; * With Cobalt, m1; p244; m1; k marked st; m1; p 180; m1; k marked st; rep from * once more. 860 sts.
Join in Scotch Broom and work check patt as follows —
Rnd 1: ** With Cobalt m1; * k2 Scotch Broom, k2 Cobalt; rep from * to within 2 sts of next marked st; k2 Scotch Broom; with Cobalt m1, k marked st; rep from ** to end of rnd.
Rnd 2: ** With Cobalt m1, p1; * p2 Scotch Broom, p2 Cobalt; rep from * to within 3 sts of next marked st; p2 Scotch Broom; with Cobalt p1, m1, k marked st; rep from ** to end of rnd.
Rep these last 2 rnds 3 times more working 8 check patt rnds in total and ending with 924 sts.
Break off Scotch Broom and with Cobalt k 1 rnd, increasing 1 st at each side of marked sts as set. 932 sts. Cast off purlwise.

FINISHING

Trim steeks to a 2st width. With Cobalt, cross stitch steeks in position. Darn in loose ends. Press lightly on WS, using a warm iron and damp cloth, omitting edging. Alternatively, rinse, spin and block out to measurements.

KEY

■	COBALT
□	SEABRIGHT
●	TURQUOISE
	CREAM
◆	CRIMSON
◇	PALE TURQUOISE
▲	FORGET-ME-NOT
✳	CAMPBELL RED
+	RYE
╱	SCOTCH BROOM
◡	PUMPKIN

CHART

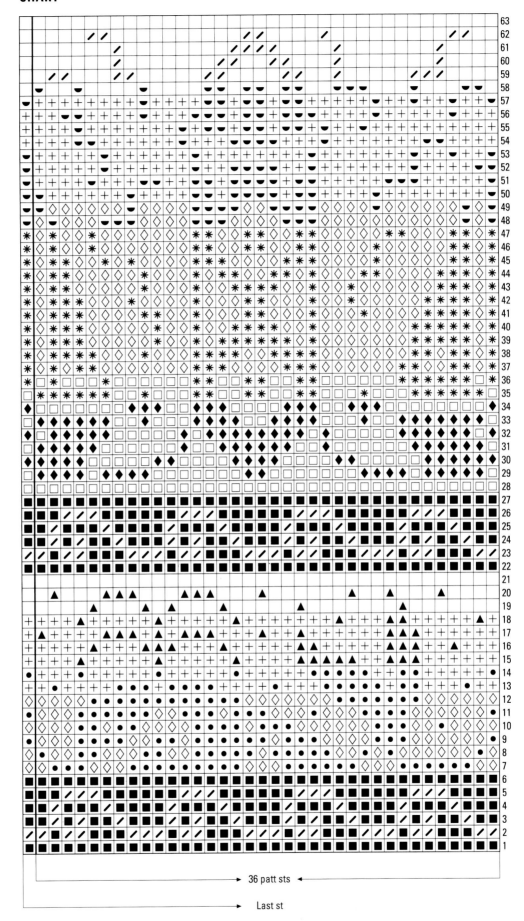

36 patt sts

Last st

Point Arena

SIZES

To fit bust 86-91[97-102,107-112]cm
34-36[38-40,42-44]in. Directions for larger sizes are given in square brackets. Where there is only one set of figures, it applies to all sizes.

KNITTED MEASUREMENTS

Underarm 116[122,129]cm 45.5[48,50.5]in.
Length 69[71,74]cm.
Sleeve length (cuff to armhole) 41[42,43]cm.

MATERIALS

10[11,12] Skeins of **Bainin,** shown in Slate and Navy.
1 Pair each 4mm (US 6) and 5mm (US 8) needles.
1 Set of double-pointed or short circular 4mm (US 6) needles. Cable needle. 4 Stitch holders.

STITCHES

Chart Patt: All odd numbered rows are RS and are read from right to left. All even numbered rows are WS and are read from left to right.

TENSION

24 Sts and 28 rows to 10cm, measured over chart patt using 5mm (US 8) needles. To make an accurate tension swatch, cast on 35 sts. Work from row 1 of chart and rep the 8 patt sts 4 times, then patt the last 3 sts as indicated. Do not press swatch. To measure, pin swatch down on a flat surface, keeping side edges straight.

FRONT

** With 5mm (US 8) needles, cast on 139[147,155] sts. Set the patt as follows—
Foundation Row 1 (RS): P1; * k1; p2; k3; p2; rep from * to the last 2 sts; k1; p1.
Foundation Row 2 (WS): * P3; k1; rep from * to the last 3 sts; p3.
Beg at row 1 of chart and work the patt as follows—
Row 1 (RS): Reading from right to left, rep the 8 patt sts 17[18,19] times; patt the last 3 sts as indicated.
Row 2 (WS): Reading from left to right, patt the first 3 sts as indicated; rep the 8 patt sts 17[18,19] times.
Continue as set and rep the 4 rows of chart until front measures 44[45,47]cm from cast on edge, with RS facing for next row.
Shape Armhole
Keeping continuity of patt, cast off 10 sts at beg of next 2 rows, decreasing 1 st over cable during cast off.
Shape raglan as follows—
Next Row (RS): Beg at third st of chart and patt the first 5 sts as set; p2tog; keeping continuity, patt to the last 7 sts; p2tog; keeping continuity, patt the last 5 sts as set, ending on third last st of chart.
Next Row (WS): Keeping continuity, patt as set and k the

6th and 6th last st from decrease on previous row. ***
Rep these 2 rows until 65[71,75] sts remain. Patt the next WS row.
Next Row – Beg Front Neck Shaping
With RS facing, patt the first 5 sts as set; p2tog; keeping continuity, patt the next 12 sts; place the next 27[33,37] sts on a holder; leave the rem 19 sts on a spare needle. Turn, and keeping continuity of patt throughout, shape left side of neck as follows—
+ Dec 1 st at neck edge of next and every foll alt row and AT THE SAME TIME, continue to dec at raglan on RS rows as set until 5 sts rem.
Next Row (RS): P1; (k2tog) twice. 3sts.
Next Row (WS): Sl1-p2tog-psso. Break yarn and fasten off.
++
With RS facing, rejoin yarn to the 19 sts of right side and keeping continuity, patt the first 12 sts; p2tog; keeping continuity, patt the last 5 sts. Turn and shape right side of neck as left from + to ++.

BACK

As front from ** to ***. Rep these 2 rows until 49[55,59] sts rem. patt the next WS row. Break off yarn and place sts on a holder.

SLEEVES

With 4mm (US 6) needles, cast on 50[50,56] sts. K1, p1 rib for 6cm, ending with WS facing for next row.
Next Row – Inc
Rib 1[1,3]; * m1, rib 6[6,5]; rep from * to the last 1[1,3] sts; m1; rib 1[1,3]. 59[59,67] sts.
Change to 5mm (US 8) needles, beg at row 1 of chart and set the patt as follows—
Row 1 (RS): Reading from right to left, rep the 8 patt sts 7[7,8] times; patt the last 3 sts as indicated.
Row 2 (WS): Reading from left to right, patt the first 3 sts as indicated; rep the 8 patt sts 7[7,8] times.
Continue as set and inc 1 st at each end of next and every foll 3rd row, working all inc sts into patt, until there are 123[123,131] sts. Continue in patt without shaping until sleeve measures 41[42,43]cm from cast on edge, with RS facing for next row.
Shape Armhole
Keeping continuity, cast off 10 sts at beg of next 2 rows, decreasing 1 st over cable during cast off.
Work the 2 raglan shaping rows as front and back until 33[31,35] sts rem. Break off yarn and place sts on a holder.

FINISHING

Do not press. Block out pieces to measurements shown on schematic. Sew sleeves to back and front at raglan and armholes. Sew up side and sleeve seams, leaving 15cm open at each side. Do not press seams.
Collar
With RS facing, set of double-pointed or circular 4mm (US 6) needles, beg at back neck holder and pick up and k the 49[55,59] sts from holder; pick up and k the 33[31,35] sts

from left sleeve holder; knit up 15 sts evenly along left side of neck; pick up and k the 27[33,37] sts from front neck holder; knit up 15 sts evenly along right side of neck; pick up and k the 33[31,35] sts from right sleeve holder. 172[180,196] sts.

Next Rnd – Dec
* K1, k2tog; rep from * to the last 4[0,4] sts; k 4[0,4]. 116[120,132] sts.
Place a marker at beg of rnd and work k1, p1 rib for 6cm.
Second Size: Work 1 more rnd of rib and inc 2 sts evenly across the back, and 1 st at centre of each sleeve during the rnd. 124 sts.

All Sizes – Divide Collar
Work k1, p1 rib to st at centre front neck and cast off this st. 115[123,131] sts. The next st is now the beg of the WS patt rows. Patt as follows—
Row 1 (WS): Reading from left to right, beg at row 4 of chart and patt the first 3 sts as indicated, then rep the 8 patt sts 14[15,16] times.
Row 2 (RS): Reading from right to left, beg at row 1 and rep the 8 patt sts 14[15,16] times, then patt the last 3 sts as indicated. Work 21 chart patt rows in total. Cast off sts in patt. Darn in loose ends.

CHART

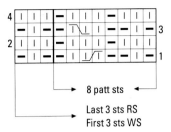

8 patt sts

Last 3 sts RS
First 3 sts WS

KEY

⊟ p on RS rows; k on WS rows.

☐ k on RS rows; p on WS rows.

sl first st to cn and hold at back; k1; k1 from cn.

sl first st to cn and hold at front; k1; k1 from cn.

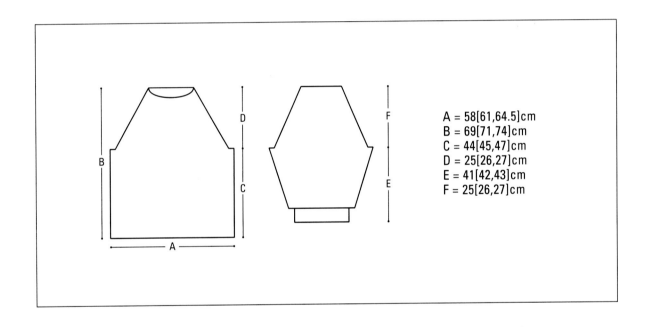

A = 58[61,64.5]cm
B = 69[71,74]cm
C = 44[45,47]cm
D = 25[26,27]cm
E = 41[42,43]cm
F = 25[26,27]cm

Irish Beach

SIZES

To fit chest/bust 81-86[91-99,102-107]cm
32-34[36-39,40-42]in. Directions for larger sizes are given in square brackets. Where there is only one set of figures, it applies to all sizes.

KNITTED MEASUREMENTS

Underarm 109[116,125]cm 43[46,49]in.
Length 66[68,70]cm.
Sleeve length 44cm.

MATERIALS

13[14,15] Skeins of **Scottish Heather** shown in Sholmit/ Mooskit and Amethyst.
1 Pair of 4mm (US 6), 4.5mm (US 7) and 5mm (US 8) needles. 1 Set of double-pointed or short circular 4.5mm (US 7) needles. 1 Cable needle. 4 Stitch holders.

STITCHES

Moss Stitch: Worked over an even number of stitches as follows—
Row 1(RS) * K1, p1; rep from * to end of row. **Row 2:** As row 1. **Rows 3 & 4:** * P1, k1; rep from * to end of row. Rep rows 1 – 4. **Chart Patt:** Odd numbered rows are RS and are read from right to left. Even numbered rows are WS and are read from left to right.

TENSION

22 Sts and 28 rows to 10cm, measured over Moss Stitch, using 4.5mm (US 7) needles.

FRONT

** With 5mm (US 8) needles, cast on 158[170,182] sts. Reading RS rows from right to left, and WS rows from left to right, beg at row 1 of chart and set the patt as follows—
Row 1 (RS): Patt the first st as indicated; rep the 12 patt sts 13[14,15] times; patt the last st as indicated.
Continue as set and rep the 8 patt rows 5 times in all. 40 rows. Work through row 7 once more. 47 rows. Change to 4.5mm (US 7) needles.
Next Row (WS) – Dec
First & Third Sizes: P2; * (p2tog) twice; p1; p2tog; p5; rep from * to the last 12 sts; (p2tog) twice; p8. 120[138] sts.
Second Size: P2 * (p2tog) twice; p1; p2tog; p5; rep from * to end of row. 128 sts.
All Sizes
Beg at row 1 and rep the 4 patt rows of Moss Stitch until front measures 30[31,32]cm from cast on edge, ending with WS facing for next row.
Work Ridge Patt
+ Change to 4mm (US 6) needles. **Row 1 (WS):** Purl. **Row 2 (RS):** Purl. **Row 3 (WS):** Knit. **Row 4 (RS):** Knit. **Row 5 (WS):** Purl. **Row 6 (RS):** Purl. **Row 7 (WS):** Knit. **Row 8 (RS):** Knit.

Change to 4.5mm (US 7) needles. With WS facing work row 4 of Moss Stitch patt. Beg at row 1 and continue in Moss Stitch until front measures 42[43,44]cm from cast on edge, with WS facing for next row. ++
Rep from + to ++ once more until front measures 54[55,56]cm from cast on edge, with WS facing for next row. Change to 4mm (US 6) needles and work the 8 rows of ridge patt once more. ***
Change to 4.5mm (US 7) needles and continue in Moss Stitch as before until front measures 57.5[59.5,61.5]cm from cast on edge, with RS facing for next row.
Front Neck Shaping
Work Moss Stitch as set over the first 47[51,56] sts; place the next 26 sts on a holder; leave the rem sts on a spare needle. Turn and keeping continuity, shape left side of neck as follows—
+ Dec 1 st at neck edge of next 2 rows. Patt 1 row without shaping, then dec 1 st at neck edge of next and every foll alt row 7 times in all. 38[42,47] sts rem. Patt 2 rows without shaping, thus ending with WS facing for next row. Change to 4mm (US 6) needles and work the first 4 rows of ridge patt. Place sts on a holder. ++
With RS facing, rejoin yarn to the sts of right side and keeping continuity, patt to end of row. Then work as left side from + to ++.

BACK

As front from ** to ***. Continue in Moss Stitch until back matches front in length to 1 row below last row of Moss Stitch on front shoulders, thus ending with RS facing for next row.
Shape Back Neck
Work Moss Stitch as set over the first 39[43,48] sts; place the next 42 sts on a holder; leave the rem sts on a spare needle. Turn and work right side of neck as follows—
+ Change to 4mm (US 6) needles and work row 1 of ridge patt, decreasing 1 st at neck edge of row. 38[42,47] sts. Work rows 2 through 4 of ridge patt. Place sts on a holder. ++
With RS facing and 4.5mm (US 7) needles, rejoin yarn to the sts of left side and keeping continuity, patt as set to end of row. Work as right side from + to ++.
Place front and back shoulder sts on needles with points at sleeve edge. With right sides of back and front together, hold shoulder sts parallel, and with a third needle, cast off shoulder sts together on WS, working from sleeve to neck edge.

SLEEVES

With 4.5mm (US 7) needles, cast on 62 sts. Reading RS rows from right to left, and WS rows from left to right, beg at row 1 and work the patt from chart as follows—
Row 1 (RS): Patt the first st as indicated; rep the 12 patt sts 5 times; patt the last st as indicated.
Continue as set and rep the 8 patt rows 3 times. 24 rows. Beg with a RS row and continue in Moss Stitch, shaping sleeve as follows—
First & Second Sizes: Working all inc sts into Moss Stitch,

inc 1 st at each end of 7th[first] row. Patt 3 rows without
shaping then inc as set on next and every foll 4th row.
Third Size: Working all inc sts into Moss Stitch, inc 1 st at
each end of 3rd and every foll 3rd row until there are 82
sts, then continue to inc as set on every foll 4th row.
All Sizes
Continue to work in Moss Stitch and inc as set until sleeve
measures 32cm from cast on edge, with WS facing for next
row. Then change to 4mm (US 6) needles and continue to
inc as set and work the 8 rows of ridge patt. WS facing for
next row. Change to 4.5mm (US 7) needles and work row
4 of Moss Stitch patt, then working from row 1, continue in
Moss Stitch and inc as set until there are 106[110,114] sts.
Continue in Moss Stitch without further shaping until sleeve
measures 43cm, with WS facing for next row. Change to
4mm (US 6) needles and work the first 4 rows of ridge patt.
With WS facing, cast off purlwise.

FINISHING

Do not press. Block out to measurements shown on schematic. Place centre top of sleeve at shoulder cast off, and
place each top end of sleeve at centre of second ridge of
back and front. Pin and sew sleeves to body. Using a warm
iron and damp cloth, press seams very lightly on WS. Sew
up side and sleeve seams and press seams as before, omitting cabled areas.
Collar
With RS facing, double-pointed or circular 4.5mm (US 7)
needles, beg at back neck holder and pick up and inc as follows—
K3; (m1,k5) 7 times; m1; k4; – 50 sts; knit up 25 sts evenly
along left side of neck; pick up and inc from front neck
holder as follows—
K1; (m1,k5) twice; m1; k4; (m1,k5) twice; m1; k1 – 32 sts;
knit up 25 sts evenly along right side of neck to complete
the rnd. 132 sts.
Place a marker at beg of rnd, and reading all rows of chart
from right to left (all rnds are RS), rep the 12 patt sts 11
times in the rnd. Rep the 8 patt rnds 3 times. 24 Rnds.
Cast off knitwise decreasing during cast off as follows—
* Cast off 5; k2tog and cast off; cast off 1; (k2tog and cast
off) twice; rep from * to end of rnd. Darn in loose ends.

CHART

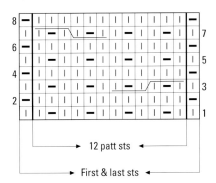

KEY

⊟ p on RS rows; k on WS rows.

□ k on RS rows; p on WS rows.

sl first 3 sts to cn
and hold at back; k1, p1, k1; then
k1, p1, k1 from cn.

sl first 3 sts to cn
and hold at front; k1, p1, k1; then
k1, p1, k1 from cn.

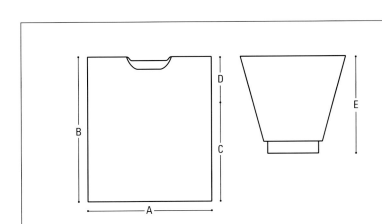

A = 54.5[58,62.5]cm
B = 66[68,70]cm
C = 42[43,44]cm
D = 24[25,26]cm
E = 44cm

Mendocino

SIZES

To fit chest/bust 81-89[91-99,102-112]cm
32-35[36-39,40-42]in.
Directions for larger sizes are given in square brackets. Where there is only one set of figures, it applies to all sizes.

KNITTED MEASUREMENTS

Underarm (buttoned) 113[121,129]cm 44.5[47.5,51]in.
Length 70[73,76]cm.
Sleeve length 44[45,46]cm.

MATERIALS

9[10,11] Skeins of **Bainin**, shown in Ruby and Lichen.
1 pair each 4.5mm (US 7) and 5mm (US 8) needles.
1 Cable needle. 5 Stitch holders. Stitch markers. 10 Buttons.

STITCHES

Moss Stitch: Worked over an odd number of sts as follows—
Rows 1 & 4: * K1, p1: rep from * to the last st; k1. **Rows 2 & 3:** * P1, k1; rep from * to the last st; p1. Rep rows 1 – 4.
St.st: K all RS rows and p all WS rows. **Chart Patts:** All odd numbered rows are RS and are read from right to left. All even numbered rows are WS and are read from left to right.

TENSION

19 Sts and 24 rows to 10cm, measured over st.st. using 5mm (US 6) needles.

RIGHT FRONT

With 5mm (US 8) needles, cast on 45[49,53] sts. Work 8 rows of Moss Stitch.
Next Row (RS) – Inc
K 3[2,1]; * m1, k 7[8,9]; rep from * 5 times in all; m1; work Moss stitch as set over the last 7 sts. 51[55,59] sts.
Set patt as follows—
Row 1 (WS): Work Moss Stitch as set over the first 7 sts; p to end of row.
Row 2 (RS): K to the last 7 sts; work Moss Stitch as set over the last 7 sts.
Rep these 2 rows until front measures 10cm from cast on edge, with WS facing for next row. Beginning with a p row, work all foll rows in st.st. until front measures 40[42,44]cm from cast on edge, with RS facing for next row.
Set Right Yoke Patt
Row 1 (RS): K1; reading the chart from right to left, rep the 8 patt sts 3 times over the next 24 sts; patt the last 3 sts as indicated; k 23[27,31].
Row 2 (WS): P 23[27,31]; reading the chart from left to right, patt the first 3 sts as indicated; rep the 8 patt sts 3 times over the next 24 sts; p1.
Continue as set, working through row 10 of chart once only. Thereafter, rep rows 7 through 10 and continue until

front measures 63[65,68]cm from cast on edge, with RS facing for next row.
Shape Front Neck
+ Patt the first 8 sts and place these sts on a holder; keeping continuity, patt to end of row. Keeping continuity throughout, dec 1 st at neck edge of next row; cast off 3[3,4] sts at beg of next row; dec 1 st at neck edge of next and every foll alt row 5[6,6] times in all. 34[37,40] sts rem. **++**
Patt 1 row without shaping. Cast off all sts in patt and dec 2 sts evenly over cable during cast off.

LEFT FRONT

Cast on 45[49,53] sts and work 8 rows of Moss Stitch as right front.
Next Row (RS) – Inc
Work Moss Stitch as set over the first 7 sts; * m1, k 7[8,9]; rep from * to the last 3 [2,1] sts; m1; k 3[2,1]. 51[55,59] sts. Continue as right front, but working Moss Stitch edging at right side as set in the previous row. Work edging and change to st.st as right front and continue until left front matches right front in length to beg of yoke patt, with RS facing for next row.
Set Left Yoke Patt
Row 1 (RS): K 23[27,31]; reading the chart from right to left, rep the 8 patt sts 3 times over the next 24 sts; patt the last 3 sts as indicated; k1.
Row 2 (WS): P1; reading the chart from left to right, patt the first 3 sts as indicated; rep the 8 patt sts 3 times over the next 24 sts; p 23[27,31].
Continue as set and work the chart rows in the same sequence as right front and continue as set until left front matches right in length, plus 1 extra row, thus ending with WS facing for next row. Shape left neck as right, from **+** to **++**. Cast off all sts in patt, decreasing 2 sts evenly over cable during cast off.

BACK

With 5mm (US 8) needles, cast on 95[103,111] sts. Work Moss Stitch for 8 rows.
Next Row (RS) – Inc
Work Moss Stitch as set over the first 7 sts; k 0[4,3]; * m1, k 9[9,10]; rep from * 9 times in all; m1; k 0[4,4]; work Moss Stitch as set over the last 7 sts. 105[113,121] sts.
Beg with a WS row, work Moss stitch as set over the first and last 7 sts, and work st.st. over the inside 91[99,107] sts until back measures 10cm from cast on edge, with WS facing for next row.
Beg with a p row and continue in st.st. over all sts until back matches fronts in length to beg of yoke patt, with RS facing for next row.
Set Back Yoke Patt
Row 1 (RS): K 23[27,31]; reading the chart from right to left, rep the 8 patt sts 7 times over the next 56 sts; patt the last 3 sts as indicated; k 23[27,31].
Row 2 (WS): P 23[27,31]; Reading the chart from left to right, patt the first 3 sts as indicated; rep the 8 patt sts 7 times over the next 56 sts; p 23[27,31].
Continue as set, working the chart rows in the same se-

quence as fronts, until back matches fronts in length at shoulder cast off edge, with RS facing for next row.

Shape Shoulders

Cast off 34[37,40] sts in patt at beg of next 2 rows, decreasing 2 sts over each cable during cast off. Place the centre back 37[39,41] sts on a holder.

SLEEVES

With 4.5mm (US 7) needles, cast on 46[48,50] sts. Work k1,p1 rib for 6cm, with WS facing for next row.

Next Row – Inc

Rib 1[2,1]; * m1, rib 11[11,12]; rep from * to the last 1[2,1] sts; m1; rib 1[2,1]. 51[53,55] sts.
Change to 5mm (US 8) needles and beg with a RS row, work all sts in st.st., increasing 1 st at each end of every 3rd row until there are 67[71,77] sts. Then continue as set and inc on every foll 4th row until sleeve measures 34[35,36]cm from cast on edge, with RS facing for next row.

Set Chart Patt

Working st.st. at each side, set the chart patt as fronts over the centre 27 sts of sleeve. Work the same chart row sequence as fronts and back, and continue to inc on every 4th row as set, until there are 99[103,107] sts. Then continue in patt without further shaping, until sleeve measures 44[45,46] cm from cast on edge, with RS facing for next row.

Shape Saddle

Cast off 45[47,49] sts in patt at beg of next 2 rows, decreasing 2 sts evenly over each cable during cast off. 9 centre sleeve sts rem.
Continue in patt as set over the 9 sts, until saddle fits in length along shoulder cast off edge. Place sts on a holder.

FINISHING

Using a warm iron and a damp cloth, press WS of st.st. area of each piece. Do not press cabled areas, thus allowing cable patt to gather shape in gently on yokes and sleeves. Place markers 22[23,24]cm down from shoulder cast off edge on back and fronts. Sew saddles along shoulder cast off edges of back and fronts. Sew cast off edges of sleeves to back and fronts between markers. Press seams very lightly on WS – avoid pressing on cable areas.
Sew up sleeve seams. Sew up side seams above Moss Stitch edgings. Press seams very lightly on WS, omitting ribs.

Collar

With RS facing and 4.5mm (US 7) needles, beg at right front and pick up and k the 8 sts from holder and dec 1 st at centre of cable; knit up 13[14,15] sts evenly along right side of neck; pick up and k the 9 sts from right saddle and dec 1 st at centre of cable; pick up and k the 37[39,41] sts from back neck holder and dec 1 st at centre of first 2 and last 2 cables – 33[35,37] sts rem from holder; pick up and dec 1 st from left saddle as right; knit up 13[14,15] sts evenly along left front neck; pick up and dec 1 st from left front holder as right. 89[93,97] sts.
Rib as follows—
Row 1 (WS): K1; * p1, k1; rep from * to end of row.
Row 2 (RS): P1 * k1, p1; rep from * to end of row.

Rep these 2 rows and work 8[8,10] rows in total. Change to 5mm (US 8) needles and work 23 rows of Moss Stitch. Cast off in patt.

Button Band

With 4.5mm needles, cast on 7 sts. Work Moss Stitch until band, when slightly stretched, fits along left front edge to beg of collar rib. Cast off sts. Pin and sew band to front edge. Mark position of 10 buttons on button band with pins, to ensure even spacing, the first to come 7cm from cast on edge, the last to come 1.5 cm from cast off edge, with the remainder spaced evenly between.

Buttonhole Band

Work as button band with the addition of 10 buttonholes, worked to correspond with markers on button band. Work buttonhole as follows—
Buttonhole Row: Moss stitch 3; yo; patt 2tog; Moss Stitch 2. Pin and stitch band in position as button band, Press seams very lightly on WS, taking care not to press on yoke cables. Sew buttons onto button band.

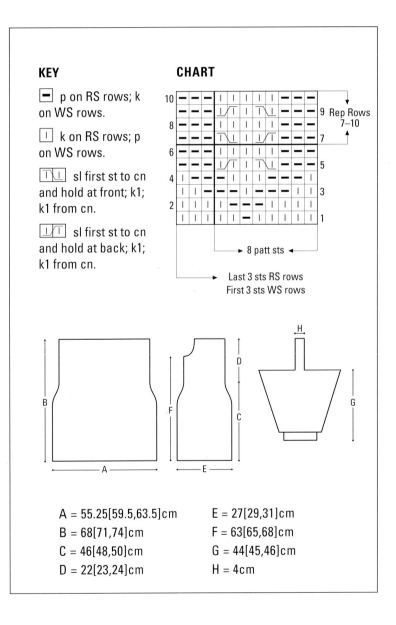

KEY

□ - p on RS rows; k on WS rows.

□ | k on RS rows; p on WS rows.

sl first st to cn and hold at front; k1; k1 from cn.

sl first st to cn and hold at back; k1; k1 from cn.

CHART

Rep Rows 7–10

→ 8 patt sts ←

→ Last 3 sts RS rows
First 3 sts WS rows

A = 55.25[59.5,63.5]cm
B = 68[71,74]cm
C = 46[48,50]cm
D = 22[23,24]cm

E = 27[29,31]cm
F = 63[65,68]cm
G = 44[45,46]cm
H = 4cm

MENDOCINO SHOWN IN RUBY

CABLED BACK–YOKE PATTERN

Super Skunk

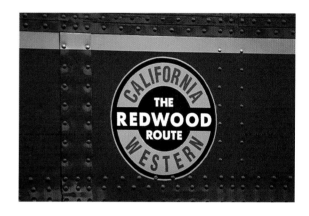

SIZES

To fit approx age 2-3[4-5,6-7] years, or —
chest 54-56[58-61,63-66]cm 21-22[23-24,25-26]in.
Directions for larger sizes are given in square brackets.
Where there is only one set of figures, it applies to all sizes.

KNITTED MEASUREMENTS

Underarm (buttoned) 67[72,77.5]cm 26.5[28.5,30.5]in.
Length 32[37,41.5]cm.

MATERIALS

Of **Scottish Campion**—
1[1,2] Skeins of Ruby.
1 Skein each of Ginger, Night Hawk, Brick, Claret, Evergreen, Spruce, Aegean and Loganberry.
1 Set of double-pointed or circular 3.25mm (US 3) needles.
3 Stitch holders. Stitch markers. 5[5,6] buttons.

STITCHES

Check Patt: K2 with first colour, k2 with second colour, stranding the yarns evenly across the WS. On flat rows every row is worked in k, and on circular rnds every alt rnd is worked in p. It is important to remember to strand the yarn on the WS after every p2. **Chart Patt:** All rnds are read from right to left. K every rnd, stranding the yarn not in immediate use evenly across the WS. **Steeks:** Worked at front, armholes and neck and later cut up centre to form openings. Each steek is worked over 8 sts and k on every rnd. On two-colour rnds, the steek sts are worked in alt colours on every st and rnd. Do not weave in newly joined in or broken off yarns at centre of front steek. Instead leave approx 5cm tail when joining in and breaking off yarns. **Edge Stitch:** Worked at each side of steeks and k in background colours throughout. Sts for front and armhole bands are knitted up from edge st. **Cross Stitch:** With darning needle, overcast raw edges of trimmed steeks to strands on WS, and after sewing to end, reverse to form cross stitches.

TENSION

30 Sts and 34 rows to 10cm, measured over chart patt using 3.25mm (US 3) needles. To make an accurate tension swatch, cast on 32 sts on 1 double-pointed or circular needle and work a flat piece, **knitting on the RS only**, breaking off the yarns at the end of every row. Reading from right to left work the first 32 sts of chart and work the 28 rows. Then work rows 1 through 12 once more.

BODY

With 3.25mm (US 3) needles and Ruby, cast on 192[208,224] sts. Place a marker at beg of rnd and joining in and breaking off colours as required, join in Ginger and set the front steek, edge sts and check patt as follows—
Rnd 1: With alt colours, k4 steek sts; with Ruby, k1 edge st; * k2 Ginger, k2 Ruby; rep from * to the last 7 sts; k2 Ginger; with Ruby, k1 edge st; with alt colours k4 steek sts.
Rnd 2: With alt colours k4 steek sts; with Ruby k1 edge st; * p2 Ginger, p2 Ruby; rep from * to the last 7 sts; p2 Ginger; with Ruby k1 edge st; with alt colours, k4 steek sts.
Rnds 3 & 4: As rnds 1 & 2, substituting Night Hawk for Ruby and Brick for Ginger.
Rnds 5 & 6: As set, substituting Claret for Night Hawk and Evergreen for Brick.
Third Size Only: Work two more rnds swapping Claret and Evergreen over steek and check patt sts.
All Sizes – Next 2 Rnds: As set, substituting Night Hawk for Claret and Brick for Evergreen. Break off yarns.
Next Rnd – Inc
With Ruby, k 10[9,8]; * m1, k 19[21,23]; rep from * to the last 11[10,9] sts; m1; k 11[10,9]. 202[218,234] sts.
Next Rnd – Beg Chart Patt
Join in Ginger and with alt colours, k4 steek sts; with Ruby k1 edge st; reading from right to left, beg at row 1 and patt the first 16 sts as indicated; rep the 16 patt sts 10[11,12] times; patt the last 16 sts as indicated; with Ruby k1 edge st; with alt colours k4 steek sts.
Joining in and breaking off colours as required, continue as set, working edge sts in background colours throughout, and steek sts in alt colours on two-colour rnds. Rep the 28 patt rnds and work 50[60,69] patt rnds in total, thus ending on rnd 22[4,13] inclusive.
Next Rnd – Beg V Neck Shaping
With alt colours as for next rnd of chart, k4 steek sts; k1 edge st; ssk; keeping continuity, patt as set to the last 7 sts; k2 tog; k1 edge st; k4 steek sts.
Place a marker on each edge st to mark beg of V neck shaping.
Keeping continuity, patt the next rnd without shaping.
Next Rnd – Beg Armhole Shaping
With colours as next rnd of chart, k4 steek sts and k1 edge st as set; keeping continuity, patt the next 39[42,45] sts (right front); place the next 11[13,15] sts on a holder; cast on 10 edge and steek sts (using alt colours for 8 centre steek sts on first and second sizes); keeping continuity, patt the next 90[96,102] sts (back); place the next 11[13,15] sts on a holder; cast on 10 edge and steek sts as before; keeping continuity, patt as set to end of rnd.
Working armhole steeks and edge sts as front, and keeping continuity of patt throughout, shape V neck and armholes as follows—
Dec 1 st at chart patt side of front neck edge sts as set on next and every foll 3rd rnd. AT THE SAME TIME, dec 1 st at chart patt side of armhole edge sts on next 3 rnds, then on every foll alt rnd 4 times in all. 76[82,88] chart patt sts rem on back. Then continue in patt without further shaping at armholes and continue to dec at front neck as set on every 3rd rnd until 18[19,21] chart patt sts rem on each front, thus ending on rnd 9[25,9] inclusive.
Next Rnd – Beg Back Neck Shaping
With colours as next rnd of chart, patt as set without shaping to the 76[82,88] chart patt sts of back; patt the first 20[21,23] sts; place the next 36[40,42] sts on a holder; cast on 10 steek and edge sts, using alt colours for 8 centre steek sts; keeping continuity, patt the last 20[21,23] sts of back, then patt as set to end of rnd.

CHART

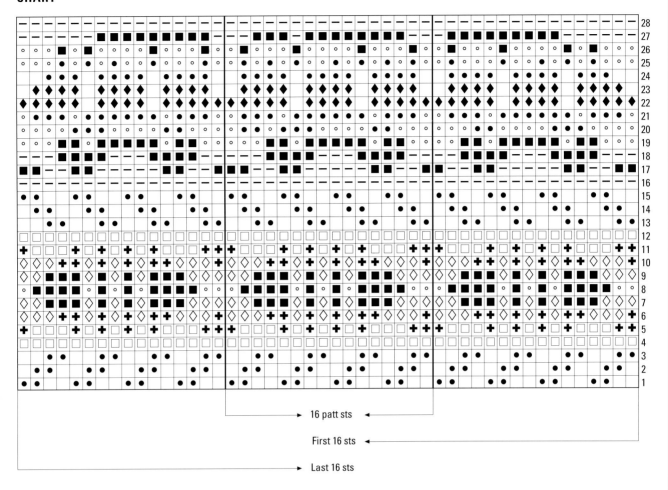

→ 16 patt sts ←

First 16 sts ←

→ Last 16 sts

KEY

●	RUBY
	GINGER
□	NIGHT HAWK
✚	BRICK
◇	EVERGREEN
■	CLARET
○	SPRUCE
—	AEGEAN
◆	LOGANBERRY

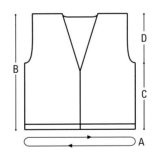

A = 67[72,77.5]cm
B = 32[37,41.5]cm
C = 18[21.5,24.5]cm
D = 14[15.5,17]cm

Working back neck steek and edge sts as front and arm-holes, continue in patt as set, working the front neck without further shaping and dec 1 st at chart patt side of back neck edge sts on next and foll alt rnd. 18[19,21] chart patt sts rem on each back shoulder. Patt 2 rnds without shaping and cast off all steek sts on last rnd.

With Ruby, graft back and front shoulder sts together including edge sts.

Front Band

Cut open front and back neck steeks up centre, between 4th and 5th steek sts. With 3.25mm (US 3) needles and Night Hawk, beg at cast on edge of right front, and working into loop of edge st next to chart patt, knit up 51[60,69] sts evenly along right front to marker at beg of V neck; knit up 48[53,55] sts evenly along right side of neck to back neck holder; pick up and k the 36[40,42] sts from back neck holder; knit up 48[53,55] sts evenly along left side of neck to V neck marker; knit up 51[60,69] sts evenly to cast on edge. 234[266,290] sts. Joining in and breaking off colours as required, work back and forth in rows and patt as follows—

Row 1 (WS): With Night Hawk, knit.

Rows 2 & 3: * K2 Night Hawk, k2 Brick; rep from * to the last 2 sts; k2 Night Hawk.

Row 4 – Make Buttonholes: K2 Claret, k2 Evergreen; * with colours as set, cast off 2, patt 9[11,10]; rep from * 4[4,5] times in all; cast off 2; continue straight in check patt to end of rnd.

Row 5: Work in patt and colours as set and cast on 2 sts over those cast off on the previous row.

Rows 6 & 7: With Night Hawk and Brick, as rows 2 & 3.

Rows 8 & 9: As set, substituting Ruby for Night Hawk and Ginger for Brick.

With Ruby, cast off purlwise.

Armhole Bands

Cut open armhole steeks up centre, between 4th and 5th steek sts.

With 3.25mm (US 3) needles and Night Hawk, beg at centre of underarm holder and pick up the last 6[7,8] sts from holder; knit up 85[95,101] sts evenly around armhole, working into loop of edge st next to chart patt; pick up and k the rem 5[6,7] sts from holder. 96[108,116] sts.

Place a marker at beg of rnd, and joining in and breaking off colours as required, work check patt as follows—

Rnd 1: * K2 Night Hawk, k2 Brick; rep from * to end of rnd.

Rnd 2: * P2 Night Hawk, p2 Brick; rep from * to end of rnd.

Rnds 3 & 4: As set, substituting Claret for Night Hawk and Evergreen for Brick.

Rnds 6 & 7: As set, with colours as rnds 1 & 2.

Rnds 8 & 9: As set, substituting Ruby for Night Hawk and Ginger for Brick.

With Ruby, cast off purlwise.

FINISHING

Trim all steeks to a 2st width and with Ruby, cross stitch steeks in position. Darn in all loose ends. Using a warm iron and damp cloth, press garment very lightly on the WS, omitting check patt areas. Sew buttons to left front band.

Noyo Harbor

SIZES

To fit chest/bust 86-94[97-104,107-114]cm
34-37[38-41,42-45]in. Directions for larger sizes are given in square brackets. Where there is only one set of figures, it applies to all sizes.

KNITTED MEASUREMENTS

Underarm 119[125,131]cm 47[49,51.5]in.
Length 67[70,73]cm.
Sleeve length 43[44,44]cm.

MATERIALS

9[10,11] Skeins of **Bainin** shown in French Blue and Ecru.
1 pair each of 4mm (US 6) and 5mm (US 8) needles. 1 Set of double-pointed or short circular 4mm (US 6) needles.
1 Cable needle. 4 Stich holders. Stitch markers.

STITCHES

Sand Stitch: Worked over an odd number of sts as follows—
Row 1 (RS): * P1, k1; rep from * to the last st; p1.
Row 2 (WS): K.
Rep these 2 rows.
Chart Patt: All odd-numbered rows are RS and are read from right to left. All even-numbered rows are WS and are read from left to right.

TENSION

20 Sts and 26 rows to 10cm, measured over Sand Stitch (see STITCHES, above) using 5mm (US 8) needles.

FRONT

** With 4mm (US 6) needles, cast on 105[109,115] sts.
Work edging as follows—
Row 1 (WS): P. **Row 2 (RS):** K. **Rows 3 & 4:** As rows 1 & 2.
Row 5. P.
Rib as follows—
Row 1 (WS): * K1, p1; rep from * to the last st; k1.
Row 2 (RS): * P1, k1; rep from * to the last st; p1.
Continue as set until rib measures 7cm with RS facing for next row.

Next Row (RS) – Inc

K 7[2,5]; * m1, k7; rep from * to the last 7[2,5] sts; m1; k 7[2,5]. 119[125,131] sts.
Change to 5mm (US 8) needles and work Sand Stitch, beginning and ending RS rows with a p1, as given in STITCHES. Continue as set until piece measures 42[44,46]cm from hemline formed by curled edging, with WS[RS,WS] facing for next row.

First and Third Sizes – Next Row (WS) – Inc

K 32[38]; m1; k55 ; m1; k 32[38]. 121[133] sts.

All Sizes – Next Row (RS) – Set Yoke Patt

Beg at row 1 of chart A, and row 1[7,1] of chart B, and reading odd-numbered (RS) rows from right to left, and even-numbered (WS) rows from left to right, set the patt over the 121[125,133] sts of front as follows—
Row 1 (RS): Work Sand Stitch as set over the first 25[27,31] sts; work chart A over the next 14 sts; work chart B over the next 43 sts; work chart A over the next 14 sts; work Sand stitch as set over the last 25[27,31] sts. ***
Continue as set and rep the chart patt rows until yoke patt measures 17[18,19]cm, with WS facing for next row.

Shape Front Neck

Patt the first 49[51,55] sts as set; place the next 23 sts on a holder; leave the rem sts on a spare needle. Turn and work right side of neck as follows—
+ Keeping continuity of patt throughout, dec 1 st at neck edge of next and every foll alt row, 9 times in all. 40[42,46] sts rem. Work 3 rows without shaping and on the last row, dec 1 st over each 3st cable and 2 sts over the 6st cable. 36[38,42] sts rem. Place sts on a holder. ++
With WS facing, rejoin yarn to the rem 49[51,55] sts on spare needle and keeping continuity, patt 1 row. Shape left side of neck as right, working from + to ++.

BACK

As front from ** to ***.
Continue as set until back matches front in length to within 1 row at shoulders, with WS facing for next row. Patt last WS row and dec over all cables as front.

Join Shoulders

Place right front shoulder sts on a needle with pointed end at sleeve edge. Hold needle with right front sts parallel with back needle, with RS of both front and back facing. With a third needle, cast off the 36[38,42] sts of right front and back shoulders together on the RS; break off yarn; place the next 41 sts of back on a holder; place the sts of left front

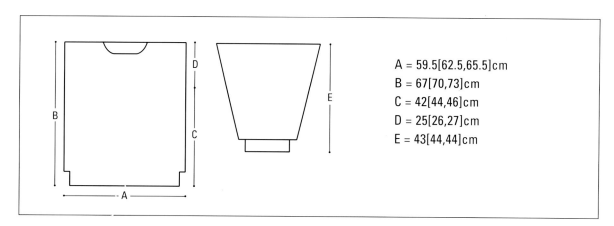

A = 59.5[62.5,65.5]cm
B = 67[70,73]cm
C = 42[44,46]cm
D = 25[26,27]cm
E = 43[44,44]cm

shoulder on a needle with the pointed end at the neck edge and with RS facing out, cast off the sts together with the left back sts as before; break off yarn.

Place markers 25[26,27]cm down from shoulder cast off at each side of back and front.

SLEEVES

With 4mm (US 6) needles, cast on 39[41,43] sts. Work 5 rows of edging as front and back.

Next Row – Inc
K 2[3,4]; * m1; k7; rep from * to the last 2[3,4] sts; m1; k 2[3,4]. 45[47,49] sts.

Work rib as back for 6cm, ending with WS facing for next row.

Next Row (WS) – Inc
Rib 1[2,3]; * m1; rib 6; rep from * to the last 2[3,4] sts; m1; rib 2[3,4]. 53[55,57] sts.

Change to 5mm (US 8) needles and work Sand Stitch, increasing 1 st at each end of 3rd and every foll 3rd row until there are 59[69,75] sts. Continue as set and inc on every foll 4th row until there are 101[105,109] sts. Continue in patt without shaping until sleeve measures 43[44,44]cm from hemline formed by curled edging. Place sts on a holder.

Join Left Sleeve to Body
With RS of body facing and 5mm needle, beg at marker on left front and knit up 50[52,54] sts evenly along left front edge to shoulder cast off; knit up 1 st from shoulder cast off; knit up 50[52,54] sts evenly along left back edge to marker. 101[105,109] sts. Place sleeve sts on a needle so that RS faces out when needle point is placed alongside body needle point. Hold needles parallel and with a third needle, cast off sleeve and body sts together on RS, working from back marker to front marker.

Join Right Sleeve to Body
Join as left sleeve, but beg knitting up body sts at back marker and work to front marker. Sts are thus cast off together on RS, working from front marker to back marker. Sew up side and sleeve seams, sewing edgings together on RS. Press seams very lightly on WS, omitting ribs.

Neckband
With RS facing and double-pointed or circular 4mm (Us 6) needles, beg at back neck holder and pick up and k the 41 sts from holder; knit up 17 sts evenly along left side of neck; pick up and k the 23 sts from front neck holder; knit up 17 sts evenly along right side of neck to complete the rnd. 98 sts. Place a marker at beg of rnd and k1, p1 rib for 5cm.

Next Rnd – Dec
* K2tog, k5; rep from * to end of rnd. 84 sts. K 5 rnds. Using a 5mm needle, cast off knitwise. Darn in loose ends.

CHART A

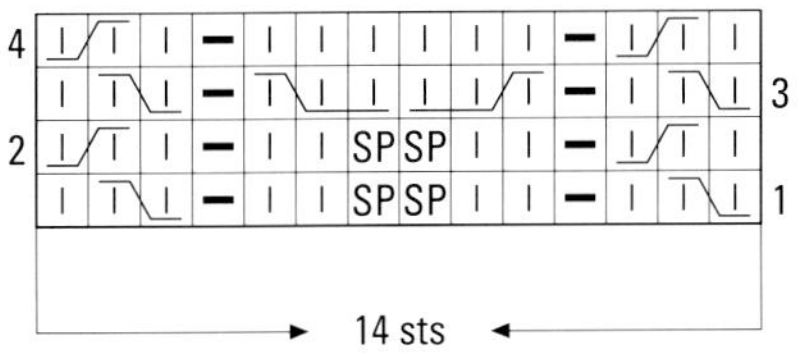

4
3
2
1

← 14 sts →

KEY

p on RS rows; k on WS rows.

k on RS rows; p on WS rows.

sl first st to cn and hold at front; k1; k1 from cn.

(WS) p into front of second st, then p into front of first st and sl both sts off needle together.

SP sl the st purlwise.

sl first 2 sts to cn and hold at back; k1; k2 from cn.

sl first st to cn and hold at front; k2; k1 from cn.

CHART B

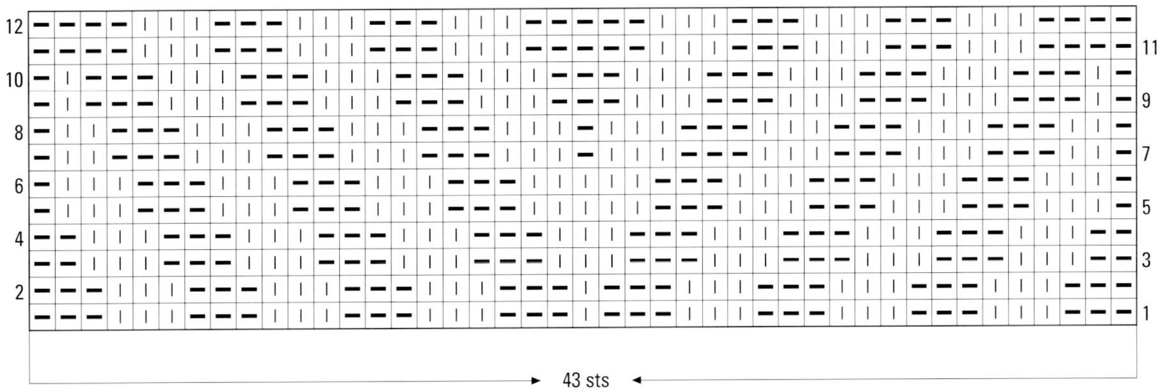

12
11
10
9
8
7
6
5
4
3
2
1

← 43 sts →

Glass
Beach

SIZES

To fit chest/bust 86-91[96-102,107-112]cm
34-36[38-40,42-44]in.
Directions for larger sizes are given in square brackets. Where there is only one set of figures, it applies to all sizes.

KNITTED MEASUREMENTS

Underarm 106.5[112,117]cm 42[44,46]in.
Length 56[59,61]cm.

MATERIALS

Of **Scottish Campion**—
3 Skeins of Ruby.
2 Skeins each of Pine and Night Hawk.
1[2,2] Skeins of Aegean.
1[1,2] Skeins of Cobalt.
1 Skein each of Leprechaun, Crimson, Violet, Thyme and Damson.
1 Set of double-pointed or circular 2.75mm (US 2) and 3.25mm (US 3) needles. 3 Stitch holders.
1 Safety pin. Stitch markers.

STITCHES

2/2 Rib: K2 with first colour, p2 with second colour, stranding the yarns evenly across the WS.
Chart Patts: All rnds are read from right to left. K every rnd stranding the yarn not immediate use evenly across the WS.
Steeks: Worked at armholes and front and back neck, and later cut up centre to form openings. Each steek is worked over 8 sts and k on every rnd. On two-colour rnds, the steeks are worked in alt colours on every st and rnd. Do not weave in newly joined in and broken off yarns at centre of first armhole steek. Instead leave approx. 5cm tail when joining in and breaking off yarns. **Edge Stitch:** Worked at each side of steeks and k in darker colour on two-colour rnds. Sts for armhole bands and neckband are knitted up from edge sts. **Cross Stitch:** With darning needle, overcast raw edges of trimmed steeks to strands on WS, and after sewing to end, reverse to form cross stitches.

TENSION

30 Sts and 34 rows to 10cm, measured over chart patt, using 3.25mm (US 3) needles. To make an accurate tension swatch, cast on 32 sts on 1 double-pointed or circular needle and work a flat piece, repeating the 16 patt sts twice, **knitting on the RS only**, breaking off the yarns at the end of every row.

BODY

With 3.25mm (US 3) needles and Night Hawk, cast on 320[336,352] sts. Place a marker at beg of rnd, and making sure cast on edge is not twisted, join in and break off colours as required and work 2/2 rib as follows—
Rnds 1 & 2: * K2 Night Hawk, p2 Crimson; rep from * to end of rnd.
Rnd 3: * K2 Night Hawk, p2 Ruby; rep from * to end of rnd.
Rnd 4: * K2 Cobalt, p2 Ruby; rep from * to end of rnd.
Rnd 5: * K2 Cobalt, p2 Thyme; rep from * to end of rnd.
Rnds 6 & 7: * K2 Aegean, p2 Thyme; rep from * to end of rnd.
Rnd 8: As rnd 5.
Rnd 9: As rnd 4.
Rnd 10: As rnd 3.
Rnds 11 & 12: As rnds 1 & 2.
Next Rnd – Set Chart Patts
First and Third Sizes: Joining in and breaking off colours as required, beg at rnd 1 and work the patt from chart, repeating the 16 patt sts 20[22] times in the rnd.
Second Size: Joining in and breaking off colours as required, beg on 13th st of 16 st rep and working from rnd 1, work the last 4 st of rep; rep the 16 patt sts 20 times; work the first 12 sts of rep.
All Sizes: Continue as set and rep the 56 patt rnds and work 105[112,115]chart patt rnds from beg, thus ending on rnd 49[56,3] inclusive. Break off yarns.
Next Rnd – Beg Armhole Steeks and Mark Centre Front
Place the first 9[10,11] sts of rnd on a holder; with colours as for next rnd of chart patt, cast on 4 steek sts and mark the first st cast on for beg of rnd; cast on 1 edge st; keeping continuity, patt the next 71[74,77] sts; place a marker on next st (centre front) and patt this st; patt the next 71[74,77] sts; place the next 17[19,21] sts on a holder; cast on 10 sts (the first and last sts cast on are edge sts, the centre 8 are steek sts); keeping continuity, patt 143[149,155] sts (back); place the rem 8[9,10] sts of rnd on to first holder; cast on 1 edge st and 4 steek sts.
Next Rnd – Beg Armhole Shaping
With colours as for next rnd of chart, k4 steek sts; k1 edge st; ssk; keeping continuity, patt the next 139[145,151] sts of front; k2tog; k1 edge st; k8 steek sts; k1 edge st; ssk; keeping continuity, patt the next 139[145,151] sts of back; k2tog, k1 edge st; k4 steek sts.
Patt 1[3,4] more rnds as set, decreasing 1 st at chart patt side of armhole edge sts on each rnd.
Next Rnd – Beg V Neck Shaping
Working in colours as set for next rnd of chart patt, continue to dec as set at armholes, and patt to marked centre front st and place this st on a safety pin; cast on 10 steek and edge sts; keeping continuity, patt and dec as set to end of rnd.
Continue in patt, working all steeks in alt colours on two-colour rnds, and dec at armholes on next 5[3,2] rnds, then on every foll alt rnd 8 times in all (111[117,123] chart patt sts rem across back). AT THE SAME TIME, dec 1 st at chart patt side of V neck edge sts on next and foll alt rnds 16[18,18] times in all. Working without further shaping at armhole edges, continue to dec at neck edge sts on every foll 3rd rnd 10[9,10] times in all. 29[31,33] chart patt sts rem on each front shoulder. 170[180,187] chart patt rnds from beg.
Next Rnd – Beg Back Neck Shaping
With colours as for next rnd of chart, patt straight as set to the 111[117,123] chart patt sts of back; patt 32[34,36] sts; place the next 47[49,51] sts on a holder; cast on 10 steek

CHART

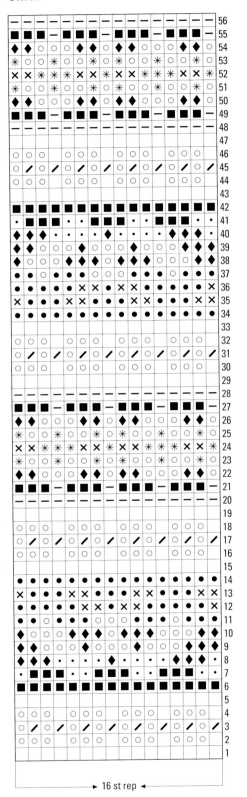

→ 16 st rep ←

KEY

	PINE
○	RUBY
╱	LEPRECHAUN
■	AEGEAN
·	THYME
◆	COBALT
●	NIGHT HAWK
✕	CRIMSON
—	DAMSON
✳	VIOLET

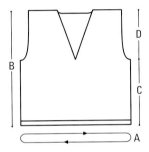

A = 106.5[112,117]cm

B = 56[59,61]cm

C = 35[37,38]cm

D = 21[22,23]cm

and edge sts; keeping continuity, patt the rem 32[34,36] sts of back and patt straight as set to end of rnd.

Working all steek and edge sts as set, and keeping continuity, dec 1 st at chart patt side of back neck edge sts on next and foll alt rnds 3 times in all. 29[31,33] chart patt sts rem on all shoulders.

First and Third Sizes: Patt 1 rnd without shaping.

All Sizes

Next Rnd – Cast off Steek sts

Working rnd 10[19,27] of chart and working edge sts as set, cast off all steek sts. Break off yarns.

With Cobalt[Pine, Damson] graft shoulder sts together including edge sts.

Neckband

Cut open back and front neck steeks up centre, between 4th and 5th steek sts. With 2.75mm (US 2) needles and Aegean, beg at centre front and working to back neck holder, knit up 70[73,76] sts evenly along right front edge st, working into loop of edge st next to chart patt sts, and mark the first st picked up for beg of rnd; pick up and k the 47[49,51] sts from back neck holder, decreasing 1 st at centre back; knit up 70[73,76] sts evenly along left neck edge st to centre front, as before; pick up and k the st from safety pin. 187[195,203] sts.

Joining in and breaking off colours as required and working 2/2 rib, shape neckband as follows—

Rnd 1: * K2 Aegean, p2 Thyme; rep from * to the last 3 sts of rnd; k1 Aegean; sl2 sts TOGETHER knitwise–k1 Aegean (first st of next rnd, move marker to next st)–p2sso.

Rnd 2: K1 Cobalt; * p2 Thyme, k2 Cobalt; rep from * to the last 4 sts; p2 Thyme; sl2 sts TOGETHER knitwise–k1 Cobalt (move marker to next st) –p2sso.

Rnd 3: * P2 Ruby, k2 Cobalt; rep from * to the last 3 sts; p1 Ruby; sl2 sts TOGETHER knitwise–k1 Cobalt (move marker to next st) –p2sso.

Rnd 4: P1 Ruby; * k2 Cobalt, p2 Ruby; rep from * to the last 4 sts; k2 Cobalt; sl2 sts TOGETHER knitwise–k1 Cobalt (move marker to next st) –p2sso.

Rnds 5 & 6: As rnds 1 & 2, but k with Night Hawk and p with Ruby.

Rnds 7 & 8: As rnds 3 & 4, but k with Night Hawk and p with Crimson.

With Night Hawk, cast off knitwise.

Armhole Bands

Cut open armhole steeks up centre, between 4th and 5th steek sts.

With 2.75mm (US 2) needles and Aegean, beg at centre st on underarm holder and pick up and k the last 9[10,11] sts from holder; mark the first st picked up (centre underarm st) for beg of rnd; knit up 131[137,143] sts evenly around armhole, working into loop of edge st next to chart patt sts; pick up and k the rem 8[9,10] sts from holder. 148[156,164] sts.

With colours as neckband work 2/2 rib for 8 rnds. Cast off knitwise.

FINISHING

Darn in all loose ends. Trim steeks to a 2st width and with Pine, cross stitch steeks in position. Press garment lightly on WS, omitting ribs, using a warm iron and damp cloth.

Broad Bay Company Stockists

ALABAMA

Yarn Expressions
7914 Memorial Parkway
Huntsville AL 35802
205–881–0260

ALASKA

Inua Wool Shoppe
202 Henderson Road
Fairbanks AK 99709
907–479–5830

Knitting Frenzy
4240 Old Seward Highway
Anchorage AK 99530
907–563–2717

CALIFORNIA

Knitting Basket
2054 Mountain Blvd
Oakland CA 94611
800–654–4887 510–339–6295

Pudding Creek Wool Co
324 North Franklin Street
Fort Bragg CA 95437
707–964–6300

Uncommon Threads
293 State Street
Los Altos CA 94022
415–941–1815

Yarn Garden
545 Sutter Street, Suite 202
San Francisco CA 94102
415–956–8830

COLORADO

Gossamer Threads & More!
575 Fourth Ave
Durango CO 81301
970–247–2822

Shuttles, Spindles & Skeins
633 South Broadway #N
Boulder CO 80303
970–494–1071

Yarns +
104 Orchard, #A2
Grand Jct CO 81501
970–245–2884

CONNECTICUT

Finally Woolies
78 North Moodus Road
Moodus CT 06469
860–873–1111

Hook 'N Needle
1869 Post Road East
Westport CT 06880
203–259–5119

FLORIDA

Cats in the Cradle
4250 Alafaya Trail
Oviedo FL 32765
407–359–7436

GEORGIA

Cast On Cottage
1003 Canton Street
Roswell GA 30075
770–998–3483

ILLINOIS

Weaving Workshop
2218 North Lincoln Ave
Chicago IL 60614
773–929–5776

The Keweenaw Shepherd
202 East Westminster Lane
Lake Forest IL 60045
847–295–9524

INDIANA

Cass Street Depot
1004 Cass Street
Fort Wayne IN 46808
219–420–2277

Mass Avenue Knit Shop
617 Massachusetts Avenue
Indianapolis IN 46204
317–638–1833

KANSAS

Knit–Wit
1815 South Ridgeview Road
Olathe KS 66062
913–780–5648

MAINE

Stitchery Square
11 Elm Street
Camden ME 04843
207–236–9773

MARYLAND

Yarns International
5110 Ridgefield Road, Suite 200
Bethesda MD 20816
800–927–6728 301–913–2980

MASSACHUSETTS

Colorful Stitches
48 Main Street
Lenox MA 01240
413–637–8206
800–413–6111

Wild & Woolly Studio
7 Meriam Street
Lexington MA 02173
617–861–7717

Woolcott & Company
61 JFK Street
Cambridge MA 02138
617–547–2837

MICHIGAN

Elegant Ewe
400 1st Street
Menominee MI 49858
906–863–2296

Inish Knits
586 East Casson Road
Maple City MI 49664
616–228–5962

The Wool & The Floss
397 Fisher Road
Grosse Pointe MI 48230
313–882–9110

Threadbender Yarn Shop
2767 44th Street SW
Wyoming MI 49509
616–531–6641

MINNESOTA

A Sheepy Yarn Shoppe
2185 Third Street
White Bear Lake MN 55110
612–426–5463
800–480–5462

NEW HAMPSHIRE

The Spinning Wheel
2 Ridge Street
Dover NH 03820
603–749–4246

The Yarn Shop & Fibres
549 Main Street
Laconia NH 03246
603–528–1221
800–375–1221

NEW JERSEY

Tomato Factory Yarn Co
8 Church Street
Lambertville NJ 08530
609–397–3475
800–483–7959

NEW MEXICO

Santa Fe Yarn & Knitting
500 North Guadalupe, Suite E
Santa Fe NM 87501
505–988–1250

Village Wools
3801 San Mateo NE
Albuquerque NM 87110
505–883–2919

NEW YORK

Garden City Stitches
725 Franklin Ave
Garden City NY 11530
516–739–KNIT(5648)

The Village Yarn Shop
200 Midtown Plaza
Rochester NY 14604
716–454–6064

NORTH CAROLINA

Keepsake Designs
120 W State Street
Black Mountain NC 28711
704–669–0600

The Yarn Studio
901 South Kings Drive #155
Charlotte NC 28204
704–374–1377

OHIO

Yarn Barn
141 East Winter Street
Delaware OH 43015
614–369–5537   800–850–6008

OKLAHOMA

Mary Jane's
6413 Avondale
Nichols Hill Plaza
Oklahoma City OK 73116
405–848–0233

OREGON

Fiber Nooks & Crannies
351 NW Jackson Ave
Corvallis OR 97330
541–754–8637

Northwest Wools
3524 SW Troy Street
Portland OR 97219
503–244–5024

Soft Horizons
412 East 13th Ave
Eugene OR 97401
541–343–0651

Web–sters
11 North Main Street
Ashland OR 97520
541–482–9801
800–482–9801

PENNSYLVANIA

Wool Gathering
131 East State Street
Kennett Square PA 19348
610–444–8236

RHODE ISLAND

A Stitch Above
190 Wayland Ave
Providence RI 02906
401–455–0269

TENNESSEE

Angel Hair Yarn Co
4121 Hillsboro Parkway #205
Nashville TN 37215
615–269–8833

UTAH

The Wooly West
1417 South 1100 East
Salt Lake City UT 84105
801–487–9378

VERMONT

Charlotte's Collections
3 Merchants Row
Middlebury VT 05753
802–388–3895

WASHINGTON

The Knit Shop
1324 Cornwall Avenue
Bellingham WA 98225
360–671–2590

Lauren's Wild & Wooly
PO Box 1719
Poulsbo WA 98370
360–779–3222
800–743–2100

The Weaving Works
4717 Brooklyn Ave NE
Seattle WA 98105
206–524–1221
Toll Free 888–524–1221

WISCONSIN

Ruhama's
420 East Silver Spring Drive
Milwaukee WI 53217
414–332–2660

The Yarn House
940 North Elm Grove Drive
Elm Grove WI 53122
414–786–5660

Canadian Stockists

ALBERTA

The Fiber Hut
2614 4th Street NW
Calgary T2M 3A1
403–230–3822

Wool Revival
6513 112 Ave
Edmonton T5W OP1
403–471–2749

BRITISH COLUMBIA

The Loom
R.R. #7; Duncan V9L 4W4
250–746–5250

Craft Cottage
7577 Elmbridge Way
Richmond V6X 2Z8
604–278–0313

Greatest Knits
1294 Gladstone Ave
Victoria V8T 1G6
604–386–5523

Patricia's Yarn Cabin
2426 Beacon Ave
Sidney V8L 1X4
604–656–4841

MANITOBA

Ram Wools
143 Smith Street
Winnipeg R3C 1J5
204–942–2797

ONTARIO

The Needle Emporium
420 Wilson Street East
Ancaster L9G 4S4
905–648–1994

The Blue Whale
3330 Simcoe Street North
Columbus L1H 7K4
905–655–8406

Rena's Yarns
6 Sydenham Street
Dundas L9H 2T4
905–627–2918

The Wool Room
2–313 University Ave
Kingston K7L 3R3
613–544–9544

The Wool Bin
236 Lakeshore Road East
Oakville L6J 1H8
905–845–9512

The Hill Knittery
10720 Yonge Street
Richmond Hill L4C 3C9
905–770–4341

The Celtic Fox
1721 Bayview Ave
Toronto M4G 3C1
416–487–8177

Passionknit Ltd
3467 Yonge Street
Toronto M4N 2N3
416–322–0688

Romni Wools
658 Queen Street West
Toronto M6J 1E6
416–703–0202

Village Yarns
4895 Dundas Street West
Toronto M9A 1B2
416–232–2361

SASKATCHEWAN

Prairie Lily
Weaving & Knitting
#7–1730 Quebec Ave
Saskatoon S7K 1V9
306–665–2771

The Wool Emporium
#7–1501 8th Street East
Saskatoon S7H 5J6
306–374–7848

UK

Jamieson Spinning (Shetland) Ltd
93–95 Commercial Street
Lerwick, Shetland ZE1 0BD
01595–693114

The buttons used for the garments in this book were hand made in lamp-worked glass by Laura Breisacher of **Origins**.
They are available to order from Broad Bay stockists in the USA.

Abbreviations

alt	alternate
approx	approximately
beg	beginning
cm	centimetre
cn	cable needle
dec	decrease
foll	following
in	inch(es)
inc	increase
k	knit
k1b	knit into the back of the stitch
m1	make one st by picking up the horizontal loop between sts and knitting into the back of it
mm	millimetre(s)
p	purl
p1b	purl into the back of the st
patt	pattern
psso	pass the slip stitch over
rem	remain(ing)
rep	repeat
rnd(s)	round(s)
RS	right side
sl	slip
ssk	slip, slip knit — slip the two sts separately knitwise, then insert the left-hand needle point through the fronts of the slipped stitches from the left, and knit them together from this position
st(s)	stitch(es)
st st	stocking stitch
tbl	through back loops
tog	together
WS	wrong side
yf	yarn forward
yo	yarn over right needle from front to back, to make a new stitch

Happy Trails